D1309274

Talking Chinese Dishes

A Selection of Recipes with Live Cooking Show Videos (QR-Coded)

by Award Winning Chef Gan Zhirong

 China Intercontinental press

 China Light Industry Press

图书在版编目（CIP）数据

会说话的中国菜：英文 / 甘智荣主编；鄢科译 . -- 北京：五洲
传播出版社，2015.4（2017.8重印）
ISBN 978-7-5085-3090-1

I . ①会… II . ①甘… ②鄢… III . ①中式菜肴—菜谱—英
文 IV . ① TS972.182

中国版本图书馆 CIP 数据核字（2015）第 052458 号

作 者：	甘智荣
策 划：	王巧丽
责任编辑：	苏 谦
助理编辑：	彭 婷
译 者：	鄢 科
审 校：	Poornima（斯里兰卡）

Talking Chinese Dishes

出版发行：五洲传播出版社
地 址：北京市海淀区北三环中路31号生产力大楼B座7层（100088）
电 话：010-82005927，010-82007837（发行部）
网 址：www.cicc.org.cn www.thatsbooks.com
开 本：16
设计承制：北京八度出版服务机构
印 刷：北京圣彩虹科技有限公司
版 次：2015年6月第1版 2017年8月第2次印刷
定 价：128.00元

Pork

Spicy Pork Strips //030

Stir-fried Cucumber with Ham Sausage //032

Stir-fried String Beans with Pork //034

Shredded Pork with Garlic Sauce //036

Stir-fried Oyster Mushrooms with Pork //038

Braised Pork with Chestnuts //040

Braised Pork with Lotus Roots //042

Braised Ribs with Potatoes //044

Steamed Ribs with Plum Sauce //046

Pork with Garlic Sauce //047

Braised Pig Feet with Preserved Bean Curd //048

Stewed Pig Feet Soup with Peanuts //050

Stir-fried Onion with Streaky Pork //052

Beef

Chili Beef //054

Stir-fried Beef with Snow Peas //056

Stir-fried Beef with Onion //058

Stir-fried Beef with Potato //060

The Nourishing Braised Beef Sirloin with Soybean //062

Braised Beef Sirloin with Turnips //064

Needle Mushrooms with Beef Rolls //066

Beef in Ginger Sauce //068

Golden Soup of Beef Rolls //069

Turnip Soup with Beef Balls //070

Mutton

Spicy Mutton with Beer //072

Mutton Steamed with Rice Flour //074

Lamb Chops with Potatoes //076

Stewed Mutton Tenderloin with Turnips //078

Stewed Mutton in Thick Soup //080

Spicy Lamb Chops //082

Poultry & Meat

Steamed Eggs with Three Delicacies //084

Fried Chicken Shreds in Assorted Colors //086

Kung Pao Chicken (spicy diced chicken with peanuts) //088

Braised Sanhuang Chicken with Pickled Chili //090

Simmered Chicken with Chestnuts //092

Stewed Rural Chicken Soup with Chestnuts //094

Stewed Rural Chicken with Ginkgo Nuts //096

Steamed Chicken with Pumpkin //098

Cola Chicken Wings //100

Simmered Chicken Wings //102

Stewed Chicken with Mushrooms //104

Sliced Chicken with Sesame //106

Stir-fried Diced Duck with Chili //107

Simmered Duck with Potatoes //108

Stewed Duck Soup with Turnips and Bamboo Fungus //110

Simmered Young Pigeons //112

Rabbit Meat Mixed with Celery //114

Chicken Shreds Mixed with Sesame Paste //116

Seafood & Fish

Shrimp mixed with Cucumber //118

Squids with Pepper Shreds //120

Stir-fried Shrimp with Pineapple //122

Baby Chinese Cabbage with Shrimp and Garlic //124

The Seething Shrimps //126

Shrimp Ball Soup with Nori //127

Fried Cuttlefish with Seasonal Vegetables //128

Cuttlefish Rolls with Green Peppers //130

Fried Squids with Young Corn Spear //132

Braised Crucian Carp //134

Braised Crucian Carp with Scallion //136

Turnip and Crucian Soup //138

Braised Mackerel //140

Steamed Bass //142

Fish Fillets in Hot Sauce //144

Fish Head Soup with Gastrodia Elata //146

Sweet and Sour Yellow Croaker //148

Winter Bamboo Shoots Soup with Seafood //150

Beans

Mapo Tofu (spicy bean curd) //152

Bean curd in Brown Sauce //154

Bean curd Balls //156

Steamed Bean curd with Shrimps //158

Vegetables

Bean Sprouts with Red Peppers //160

Purple Cabbage Mixed with Assorted Vegetables //161

Bitter Melon Mixed with Mashed Garlic //162

Smashed Cucumber Mixed with Garlic Sauce //163

Turnip Shreds in Premium Recipe //164

Stirred Snow Peas //165

Stirred Asparagus with Color Peppers //166

Fried Sliced Eggplant //167

Kung Pao Eggplant (spicy diced eggplant with peanuts) //168

Chili and Sour Shredded Potato //170

Stir-fried Corn with Color Peppers //171

Stir-fried Chinese Flowering Cabbage with Garlic //172

Braised Bamboo Shoots //174

Steamed Pumpkin with Red Dates //175

Boiled White Mushroom and Broccoli with Black Pepper //176

Jin Yu Man Tang (Prosperity of "Gold" and "Jade") //177

Deep-fried Lotus Root Sandwiches //178

Simmered Potatoes //180

Lantern Eggplant //182

Steaming Common Yam Rhizome with Lily Bulbs //183

Tomato and Spinach Soup //184

Mushrooms

Fried "Chicken-leg" Mushrooms //186

Straw Mushrooms Mixed with Celery //188

Chicken Shreds Soup with Needle Mushrooms //190

Fish Ball Soup with Two Sorts of Mushrooms //192

Sweets

Corn Congee with Chestnuts //194

Glutinous Rice Congee with Watermelon and Longan //195

Banana in Hot Toffee //196

Lucky Pumpkin Balls //198

Snow Fungus Soup with Medlar //199

Soup of Papaya, Lotus Nuts and Lily Bulbs //200

Dinnerware

When you enjoy a Chinese meal you may probably use 6 kinds of cutlery and crockery; this includes a cup, a bowl, a plate, a saucer, chopsticks and a spoon.

Cup

A cup is mainly used to serve fresh water, fruit juice, soda water or other soft drinks. Never use the cup to take liquor or wine, nor should the cup be placed upside down on the table.

Bowl

The bowl can be used to serve rice or soup. While dining, you should support the bowl of rice, with four fingers of one hand holding the bottom of the bowl and the thumb on the side of the bowl. When dining, you should hold the bowl as high as your chin.

Plate & Saucer

In a Chinese meal, you may use different kinds of plates or small saucers to serve food items. But plates should never be stacked on top of each other.
While dining, place the food that you have selected from the dishes served in the mean on the "Shidie" or the saucer. Remember never to pile too much food onto your saucer and residue, like bones or fruit-pips should be put on a seperate saucer.

Chopsticks

A pair of chopsticks is an essential part of a Chinese meal. As per the dining etiquette during a Chinese meal, the following tips should be remembered when using chopsticks:

❶ Chopsticks are used for picking food items instead of other objects, otherwise, it would be rude.

❷ When you are to talk with someone, you should put down your chopsticks, since talking while waving the chopsticks like a conductor's baton will be rude and discourteous.

❸ Never insert your chopsticks into the food and leave them up straight there (for example, stab your chopsticks into a bowl of rice and leave them up straight) , since in China, people only do this when mourning the dead.

❹ During the meal, never lick or suck your chopsticks to show how delicious the food is, because in China, people normally dine together and share food to enjoy a harmouious family atmosphere. Licking or sucking the chopsticks is not considered to be decent behavior, nor is it hygienic to do so.

Spoon

The spoon is mainly used for ladling out soup or food. Sometimes, when you use chopsticks to pick up food, you can also use a spoon to help you, however, never use a spoon alone to scoop food from a dish.

When you are not using the spoon, you should put it on the saucer in front of you. Never put it directly on the table, nor insert your spoon into a course and leave it up straight.

Chinese Culinary Art

Culinary art in China involves turning fresh ingredients into piping hot delicacies (as most cuisine is served hot, but the Chinese food culture also has cold dishes). The usual cooking styles include mixing, stir-frying, boiling, frying, simmering and stewing, etc.

Mixing

Mixing ingredients is normally used to make cold dishes like salads. During the preparation process, the fresh ingredients or cooled food that have been cooked before, are cut into tiny shreds or strips or sliced and diced or broken into chunks, etc. Different types of seasonings are mixed in and stirred evenly to finish.

Step 1.

Wash the fresh ingredients and cut them into shreds, strips, slices, dices and chunks according as per your requirements and place them on different dishes.

Step 2.

Put the fresh ingredients into boiling water and blanch them quickly, and then quickly transfer it into cold water (that has been boiled and cooled down) for a thorough cool-down, drain off the water, and place the ingredients back into their original dishes.

Step 3.

Wash garlic and shallots, and season with salt, vinegar and sesame oil and mix well before serving.

Stir-frying

Stir-frying is a widely used cooking method, with oil used as the base. The Chinese style of stir-frying involves cooking on a strong fire for a very short time and finally add seasoning to the dish.

Step 1.

Wash the ingredients and cut them into small pieces in preparation for cooking.

Step 2.

Heat the wok, add in a little oil, and then stir fry the minced shallot and ginger quickly in the hot oil.

Step 3.

Put the prepared ingredients that have been either shreded, sliced or cut into chunks, stir fry on a strong flame until the ingredients are cooked, add seasonings to finish and serve it.

Culinary Tips

❶ While stir frying, the amount of oil used depends on the quantity of ingredients used.

❷ Before starting, the wok must be pre-heated, then pour the oil, and wait till you see fumes on the oil (i.e. 60% to 70% of the oil temperature). Add the fresh ingredients.

❸ The intensity of the flame and the temperature of oil depends on the texture of the food items.

Steaming

Steaming is an important cooking method, which involves placing the ingredients in a container and cooking over steam so that the seasoned ingredients will be crispy and tender once cooked. The main advantage of this form of cooking is to maintain the original shape, taste and flavor of the food.

Step 1.

Wash the ingredients and cut them in preparation for cooking.

Step 2.

Season the fresh food items well and lay them in a dish or a bowl.

Step 3.

Put the ingredients in a steamer, and steam well on a strong flame.

Culinary Tips

❶ The main purpose of steaming is to retain the original shape, texture and freshness of the ingredients, therefore the cooked items should be fresh and natural both in terms of look and smell.

❷ Normally, a strong flame should be used when steaming. However a medium or low flame should be used when steaming fine ingredients.

❸ During the steaming process, cover the steamer but leave a small gap, so that the vapor will not condense into beads of water on the lid of the steamer and drip onto the foods?

Braising

Braising is a technique that has evolved from stewing. This involves putting pre-cooked items into a wok and adding moderate amounts of soup and seasoning and covering the wok tightly; after the content has boiled up, use a low flame and continue to heat for a long time. When the food items are cooked crispy and tender, there would be a thick gravy that has formed.

Step 1.
Wash the ingredients in preparation for cooking.

Step 2.
Stir fry the ingredients with seasonings in the wok until it gives out an aroma, and then add broth.

Step 3.
Cover the wok tight, turn on a medium or low flame to braise until the food items become tender, and then turn to strong flame to reduce the broth into gravy. Plate up once completed.

Culinary Tips
❶ Quickly boil or deep fry the cleaned and sliced ingredients.
❷ Add sufficient seasoning during the braising process and pour in enough water to cover the ingredients, and the wok must be covered tight.
❸ Usually a medium to low flame is used for a long-period for braising, so as to make the ingredients crispy and tender and produce a thick, flavourful gravy.

Intense Stewing

Intense stewing is a common method of cooking used in Chinese culinary arts. This involves preheating the ingredients for one or two times at first, and then add water for seasoning, after the broth is boiled, use a low flame to cook for a long time so that the food absorbs the flavours from the broth. Use a strong flame to reduce the broth into a thick sauce.

Step 1.

Wash the ingredients and cut well for cooking.

Step 2.

Put the ingredients in the wok and add in water to boil, then add the seasoning, and use a low flame to cook the food so that it will be rich in flavor.

Step 3.

Use a strong flame to reduce the soup into a thick sauce and season well before serving.

Culinary Tips

❶ The main ingredients need to be deep-fried, sautéd, steamed or boiled prior to stewing.
❷ Use a medium or low flame, and the cooking time depends on the texture and size of the food items.
❸ The water or the gravy needs to be reduced to a one quarter as the amount of ingredients. After cooking for a long time add starch to thicken the source if necessary.

Stewing

Stewing is a cooking method that involves adding water and seasoning to ingredients and boiling it on a strong flame at first, and then turning to a medium or low flame to go on cooking for a long time. The broth in the stew is fresh, flavourful and aromatic.

Step 1.

Wash the ingredients and cut well, and "quick-boil" (see below) in a wok.

Step 2.

Clean the wok and add some fresh water, add the pre-boiled ingredients, turn up a strong flame and bring the contents to boil, and then turn down the flame to stew the food slowly until it's crispy and tender.

Step 3.

Add seasoning to finish.

Culinary Tips

❶ During the stewing, do not add the salty seasonings first. Once the salt permeates from the food it will affect its crispness and tenderness, and you need to then extend the cooking time.

❷ Before stewing, use a strong flame to boil the broth, skim off the unwanted grease on surface, and then turn to a very small flame to stew the food until it is crispy and tender.

❸ Before stewing, it is important to add in enough water at once, and you should not add more water during the stewing, nor remove the cover from the wok.

Boiling

Boiling involves cooking food in broth or fresh water. Let the food boil on a strong flame at first, and then turn on a medium or small flame to simmer. Boiling is different from stewing, which needs less time than the latter, and is usually for the food items that are of a small size and soft texture.

Step 1.

Wash the ingredients and cut well in preparation for cooking.

Step 2.

Heat some oil in the wok, stir fry the ingredients briefly, and then add in moderate amounts of fresh water or broth, boil on a strong flame and finally turn on a medium flame to boil well.

Step 3.

Add seasoning to finish.

Culinary Tips

❶ During the boiling, do not put in too much shallot or minced ginger, or the seasoning such as cooking wine, otherwise the original taste of the broth will be affected.

❷ Don't add in too much soy sauce or add it too early, then the taste of the broth will turn sour, and the color will turn dark.

❸ Never boil too hard, then the meat will fall apart and make the broth murky.

Frying

Frying is a common cooking method. This involves adding oil to a pre-heated wok, spreading it inside the wok and then frying the ingredients until they turn golden-brown. You must constantly shake the wok while frying, so as to make the ingredients heat-up and color evenly, and to make sure that the ingredients are fully cooked. Cook until the surface of the food turns golden-brown, or even slightly burnt.

Step 1.
Wash the ingredients.

Step 2.
Pickle the ingredients before cooking.

Step 3.
Pre-heat the wok, add a little oil, and then fry the ingredients until they are fully cooked; plate up to finish.

Culinary Tips
❶ The oil should be pure; add oil in moderate amounts while frying, to avoid the burning of food.
❷ Control the flame and the period of cooking. Never use a strong flame to fry; if the oil temperature is high, the frying should be finished quickly.
❸ Season the food well; the ingredients must be pickled sufficiently, or the fried food will not be tasty.

Deep-frying

Deep-frying is a kind of cooking, where ingredients are added to plenty of hot or boiling oil, so that the food is cooked in oil. But the ingredients will become crispy and tender by deep-frying twice. The final dish would be quite savory, tender and crispy.

Step 1.

Wash the ingredients and cut well for cooking.

Step 2.

Pickle the ingredients sufficiently, or mix with starch and some water evenly.

Step 3.

Add in ingredients once the oil in the wok is heated or boiled, scoop up the food once it is fried golden-brown, and drain off the oil before plating.

Culinary Tips

❶ The ingredients for deep frying are usually pickled well first, and later placed in a dish alongside other seasoning.

❷ An important fact to keep in mind when deep frying is that the wok should contain plenty of oil.

❸ Some ingredients should be courted in flour or batter before putting them into the boiling oil.

The temperature control in Chinese style cooking

30% to 40% of the heat/oil temperature is the low oil temperature, which is around 85~120℃ ; 60% of the heat/oil temperature is the medium oil temperature, which is around 120~180 ℃ ; 80% of the heat/oil temperature is the high oil temperature, which is normally around 180~240℃ .

If the oil is stable, with no smoke and fizz, then the oil is in 30% to 40% of the oil temperature. If the oil is boiling and a slight smoke is coming out, then it is in 60% of the oil temperature; if the oil is boiling from the center to the surroundings and there is a lot of smoke, and if you stir with a ladle, there is fizz, then it is in 80% of the oil temperature.

The right way of seasoning food

When is the right moment to add seasoning? What are the right ways of seasonings that not only can give the right look, flavor and taste to a dish, but can also preserve the nutrition? Here is a brief introduction to different ways to add seasoning to your food.

Cooking oil: the hotter the better?

While stir-frying, when the oil temperature reaches above 200˚C, it will produce a harmful gas called "acrolein", which is the main component of cooking fumes, and it would also produce plenty of peroxide that tend to cause cancer. Therefore, it's better to control the oil temperature to around 80% while stir-frying.

Special Tips:

Oil and fat can weaken the effect of some antibiotics. If patients with iron deficiency or anemia eat too much oily food after taking iron supplements (e.g., ferrous sulfate), the effect of the medicine will be weakened.

We love vinegar!

When stir-frying of vegetables, if you add a few drops of vinegar after putting the vegetables in the wok, it can reduce the loss of vitamin C in vegetables, and facilitate the dissolution of calcium, phosphorus and iron, etc., so as to enhance the nutritional value of the food and enhance their ability to be absorbed by the body.

Special Tips:

Vinegar should not be applied with sulfonamides, since they tend to crystallize in the environment of acid, which will further harm the kidney; if you are taking alkalescent medicine such as sodium bicarbonate and magnesium oxide, taking vinegar will weaken the effect of such medicines.

Soy sauce: do you add it in the beginning or the end?

Allowing soy sauce to boil in a wok at a high temperature for long will damage its nutrition and deprive it of all freshness; therefore, it's better to add soy sauce only when you are ready to serve.

Special Tips:
Patients who are taking medicine to treat vascular diseases, gastrointestinal diseases or tuberculosis should not take too much soy sauce.

Sugar first, then salt.

When making the dish of Sweet-and-Sour Carp, you should put in sugar before salt, otherwise, the dehydration effect of salt would make the protein coagulate and condense, which makes it difficult for the fish to absorb sugar, and therefore it becomes "sweet outside while tasteless inside." This spoils its flavor.

Special Tips:
When eating dishes with sugar, you should never take traditional Chinese medicine decoctions at the same time, since the protein and tannin in the medicine decoction would have a chemical reaction with sugar, and further weaken the medicine effect.

Add some liquor (wine) as necessary.

Correct form is during the cooking of fish, mutton or other meat materials, it would be advisable to add some liquor, which could remove the raw smell of the materials. Therefore, the best moment to add in liquor during cooking is when the food in wok is at its highest

temperature; meanwhile, when stir-frying of shredded meat, it's better to add some liquor after the sautéing of the meat; as for cooking fish, it's better to add liquor when the fish has been fried well; regarding stir-frying shrimp meat, it's better to add liquor when the shrimp meat has been stir-fried well. If you stew some food items in soup, it would be better and normal to add in liquor when the soup has boiled up and turned to a thick sauce on a low flame.

Special Tips:

When adding liquor while cooking, you should control the amount, and always be moderate.

MSG, just a little and at the end.

When the cooking has reached a temperature of above 120°C, MSG would turn into sodium glutamate, which has not only lost its freshness, but also can be toxic; therefore, you'd better add in MSG when you are about to finish the cooking and ready to serve up.

Special Tips:

Taking too much MSG could inhibit the functions of the nervous system of the human body, which could further cause discomfort and dizziness, headaches and muscle cramps, etc. In addition, the elderly, infants and young children, nursing mothers, and people with high blood pressure or kidney disease should NOT take or take less MSG.

Salt, when and how to add it?

When cooking with soy-bean oil or rapeseed oil, in order to prevent the loss of vitamins in vegetables, it would be better to put in salt once the vegetables are stir-fried and cooked

thoroughly. If to cook with peanut oil it's better to add salt into the wok when it is being heated up at first, so as to wipe off the aspergillus flavus toxin that can be produced by the oil. If you stir frying vegetables in lard, it's better to put in a small portion of salt first, so as to kill the harmful substances left in lard; once the vegetables are cooked, add some more salt. When stir-frying of meat, it's better to add in salt when the meat has been cooked about 80%, so that the meat could become more tender.

Special Tips:

According to WHO recommendations, each person should take in 5g of salt per day, while no more than 6g. In addition, the following patients should take as less salt as possible: those who take medicine for lowering blood pressure or for dieresis, the ones who take adrenocortical hormone agents and the ones with rheumatism associated with cardiac damage.

Key points to be noted when applying seasoning.

Seasoning must be added in advance to items that have been pre-heated or are being added to the wok directly for cooking; if the ingredients are animal produce, you should add vinegar and cooking wine, so as to remove the foul smell while enhancing the flavor. During the cooking process, the seasoning should be added to the broth first, so that the ingredients can take in much more flavor from the seasoning. Add in the broth gently and slowly, pour along the wall of the wok; after the broth is boiled, stew on a medium or low flame.

Other Essential Skills

The stewing or braising time depends on the texture and shape of the ingredients.

For ingredients that are in large blocks or chunks and tough in quality, more water should be added when stewing or braising on a low flame for a long time, while the small pieces and tender ingredients can be stewed or braised with less water so that they are cooked well.

Add broth or water in moderation.

Generally speaking, the broth (or water) added in should be four times compared to the amount of the ingredients. When stewing fish, add fresh water, so as to maintain the fresh flavor of the dish, while, for stewing poultry or vegetables, add a clear broth; when stewing precious delicacies from deep mountains and seas, add thick plain soup and soup-stock.

How to reduce the broth into gravy and starch it?

Stewing to reduce the broth into gravy and adding starch to it or dressing it with starch sauce is the final part of the stewing, and is also the key part of the cooking process. After cooking for sometime, the food items have been stewed, and when the texture also meets the ideal requirements, then you need to thicken the sauce by switching on a strong flame. Make sure that the gravy (sauce) is applied evenly on the surface of the ingredients. During this stage, pay attention to the following tips:

1. Control the intensity of the flame, when stewing on a strong flame - Do not think stronger the flame the better it is for cooking.

Even when using a strong flame, there could be a slight difference: when there is plenty of broth and a few ingredients, a strong flame should be used to stew up the broth; when there is less broth, and the ingredients are tender, it would be better to stew up the broth on a medium flame, in case that the broth thickens too quickly, it would affect the quality of the food.

2. When adding starch to a soup or gravy, mix evenly and in one go. Make this the final step.

Adding starch to the stew is the final step needed to thicken the gravy. When adding starchy sauce do not stir with a spoon, since this would lead to the forming of lumps. Pour in the starchy sauce directly into the boiling broth and shake the woke well at the same time. This would ensure that the starch is mixed in evenly and is thin, without forming lumps.

3. Add some clear oil moderately.

Add some clear oil is the final step before plating up, and the amount of oil poured in will determine the look of the dishes. Pouring too much clear oil will make the dish look too shiny, however, it will also make it greasy, and it will dissolve the starchy sauce as well; if too less of the clear oil has been added, the dish will be dry and lusterless. The correct way is to pour the oil from the edge of the wok, and to shake the wok well, so that the oil can drain to the base of the wok along the edge; Shaking the wok can also make the starchy sauce and the clear oil mix together and dissolve into each other. Finally, plate up. When pouring the clear oil, it should be noted that, the food in the wok should NOT be stirred constantly after pouring the oil. This would lead to the food losing its shape or falling apart and the oil will be covered by the starchy sauce and make the dish lusterless.

Tips for retaining the nutrition in food

Although dining standards have improved in modern times, people still don't get better nutrition. Why is this? It is due to some of our unhealthy living habits that lead to the loss of nutrition in food although we are not aware of this fact. If we want to have a healthy diet and get more nutrition, we have to learn how to store and cook food in a scientific way.

Never store food for too long.

Many people like to purchase a week's food at one time and store it in the refrigerator. But actually, the longer the food is stored, the more nutrition they will loss, especially those vitamins with antioxidant effect (such as vitamin A, C, E, etc.) will be lost even more. Buy only the vegetables you need for cooking on that day and it is advisable to "buy and eat up" as opposed to storing leftovers in the fridge.

Chop meat into chunks before storing it in the refrigerator.

Some people are used to chop the thawed meat and putting the rest back into the refrigerator. Some soak the frozen meat directly in hot water to speed up the thawing, however, these are all inappropriate, for the repeated thawing and re-freezing would result in the loss of nutrition and spoil the taste as well. It would be better to chop meat into chunks and freeze in the refrigerator.

Rinse rice just twice.

Many people prefer to rinse rice three or even five times before cooking, however, the more you rinse, the more nutrition will be lost: many water-soluble vitamins will dissolve in

water, especially vitamin B1 is quite easily lost. Therefore, it's better to rinse rice with clear water just twice, and don't knead hard while washing.

Follow the culinary art principles when stir-frying.

When stir-frying, it's better to be quick with a strong flame, and never stir fry for too long. Try to add as less water as possible during the stir-frying. Add in some vinegar as needed during stir-frying. This can help to season the food and largely preserve vitamin C as well. While stir-frying meat, you can add some starch, which not only prevents the loss of nutrition, but can also make the meat more tender.

It's not suitable to heat up food for too long.

The way of cooking can also affect the level nutrition retained in the food. Leafy vegetables will loss 20%~70% of the nutrition during cooking, while over steaming and boiling would spoil the vitamins. Vitamin B, vitamin C and amino acid of high nutritive value have the same weakness that is "can't stand heat", if above 80°C, they will be spoiled. Deep frying will spoil vitamin A, C and E, and will induce the production of the toxin of acrylamide, therefore, it's not suitable to heat up food for too long.

It's not suitable to add in cold water when stewing meat.

There are many proteins and fat in meat, if you add cold water while stewing, the broth will cool down suddenly which makes the proteins and fat condense fast, while the seams between meat and bones will be narrowed − this makes it harder to stew the meat and make it tender, and the original freshness and flavor of the meat and bones will also be spoiled.

PORK

Spicy Pork Strips

Cooking Time	Taste	Culinary Art	Benefits	Suitable for
5 Minutes	Spicy	Mixing	Improve Vitality and Nourish the Blood	Female

• Ingredients
cooked pork strips 500g, red pepper 15g, peanuts 30g, white sesame seed and broccoli as needed

• Seasonings
white vinegar, salt, MSG, pepper oil, cooking oil as needed

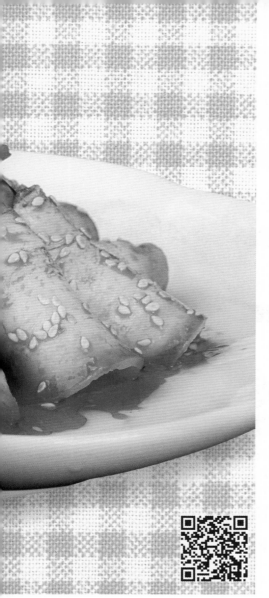

Step 1

Cut the cooked streaky pork into thin slices. Wash the red peppers and shred them.

Step 2

Pour some oil into a hot wok, and heat it up to 30% of the oil temperature. Put in the prepared peanuts, and deep fry in a low oil temperature for 2 minutes before ladling out.

Step 3

Roll up the sliced meat, and lay the rolls gently on the washed and quick-boiled broccoli, spread the peanuts on the rolls, and finally lay on the quick-boiled red pepper shreds.

Step 4

Get a bowl and add pepper oil, and add in a little white sesame seeds. Add some white vinegar, some salt and MSG to mix well.

Step 5

Serve the prepared sauce on the meat rolls and spread the rest white sesame seeds on the dish.

CULINARY TIPS

Add some salt, MSG and spices to the pork strips. This will enhance the taste.

Stir-fried Cucumber with Ham Sausage

Cooking Time	Taste	Culinary Art	Benefits	Suitable for
3 Minutes	Plain	Stir-frying	Anti-hypertension and Anti-diabetics	The Diabetic

• Ingredients
cucumber 500g, ham sausage 100g, red pepper 15g, sliced ginger, mashed garlic and chopped scallion stalk as needed

• Seasonings
salt 3g, cooking wine 3ml, oyster sauce 3g, MSG 2g, white sugar 3g, starchy sauce 10ml, cooking oil as needed

How to prepare

Step 1

Cut the peeled and cleaned cucumber into strips, and then into small sections. Cut the cleaned red pepper into half from the top and further into shreds. Cut the ham sausage into slices.

Step 2

Add some oil to the hot wok and heat up until 50%[1] of the oil temperature, Add the prepared ham sausage to stir fry even.

Step 3

Deep fry the ham sausage until it is a dark red color and then ladle out to be used later. Leave some oil and add in the sliced ginger, mashed garlic, chopped scallion stalk and red pepper to stir fry evenly. Add the prepared cucumber to stir fry briefly.

Step 4

Add the ham sausages again to stir fry together. Add in cooking wine, oyster sauce, salt, MSG, white sugar to stir fry evenly to make the food more flavourful.

Step 5

Add in some starchy sauce and stir fry quickly and evenly. Plate up to finish.

---

1 Similar as 60% of the heat/oil temperature, medium oil temperature, please refer to the previous text..

CULINARY TIPS

1. The ham sausage should not be fried for too long, if it burns it will affect the look of the dish.
2. When stir-frying the cucumber and ham sausage, never add a lot of salt.

Stir-fried String Beans with Pork

Cooking Time	Taste	Culinary Art	Benefits	Suitable for
4 Minutes	Plain	Stir-frying	Provides Protection Against Cancer	The Elderly

• Ingredients
string beans 300g, lean pork 150g, red pepper 15g, sliced ginger, mashed garlic, chopped scallion stalk as needed

• Seasonings
salt 3g, MSG 1g, starchy sauce 10ml, cooking wine, essence of chicken, oyster sauce, some baking soda and cooking oil as needed

How to prepare

Step 1

Wash the red pepper and cut into shreds. Wash the string beans and cut into small sections of about 3cm long.

Step 2

Slice the cleaned lean pork, add in some salt, MSG and baking soda to mix well. Add in starchy sauce to mix well. Add in some cooking oil, to let it marinate for about 10 minutes to add flavour.

Step 3

Heat up the oil to 40% of the oil temperature, put in the prepared string beans to stir fry for about 1 minute; ladle out the fried string beans and drain off the oil for later use.

Step 4

Add the marinated lean pork to fry until they turn white, then ladle out.

Step 5

Leave some oil in the wok, and add in the sliced ginger, mashed garlic, chopped scallion stalk and red pepper shreds to stir fry quickly to enhance the flavor. Add string beans and the cooked lean pork; add in some cooking wine to stir fry for about 2 minutes, until the meat is cooked enough; finally, add in some salt, essence of chicken, oyster sauce to stir fry until the ingredients absorb the flavour from the seasoning.

Step 6

Add in starchy sauce to dress up, and stir fry evenly. Finally, plate up.

Shredded Pork with Garlic Sauce

Cooking Time	Taste	Culinary Art	Benefits	Suitable for
2 Minutes	Sour	Stir-frying	Appetizing and Helps Digestion	General

• Ingredients
lean pork 150g, pre-soaked fungus 40g, winter bamboo shoots 100g, carrots 70g, mashed garlic, sliced ginger and garlic stalk as needed

• Seasonings
salt 3g, starchy sauce 10ml, cooking wine 5ml, MSG 3g, light soy sauce 3ml, baking soda, cooking oil, cornstarch, vinegar and thick broad-bean sauce as needed

How to prepare

Step 1

Wash the fungus and cut into shreds. Wash the carrots and slice them and further shred. Wash the winter bamboo shoots and cut into slices, and further into shreds.

Step 2

Wash the lean pork and slice them, and further cut into shreds. Add some salt, MSG and baking soda to the shredded pork and stir well. Add some starchy sauce to mix well.

Step 3

Add some cooking oil to preserve for 10 minutes to be tasty. Add some fresh water in wok and boil up with strong flame, and add in salt. Put in prepared carrots, winter bamboo shoots and fungus to boil for 1 minute to be cooked. Ladle out the boiled materials and drain off the water for use later.

Step 4

Heat up the oil to 40% of the oil temperature in the wok, put in shredded pork to fry until the flesh turn white and scoop out.

Step 5

Leave some oil in the wok, put in prepared mashed garlic, sliced ginger and garlic stalks to stir fry quickly to enhance flavor. Add carrots, winter bamboo shoots and fungus to stir fry evenly. Add in shredded pork, with cooking wine to stir fry well. Add salt, MSG, light soy sauce, thick broad-bean sauce and vinegar to stir fry well.

Step 6

Add some starchy sauce to stir fry quickly and evenly; plate up to finish.

CULINARY TIPS

Fungus should be washed clean to remove the impurities and sand, meanwhile, the fresh winter bamboo shoots are tender, and should not be over fried, otherwise, the fresh and tender taste would be spoiled.

Stir-fried Oyster Mushrooms with Pork

Cooking Time	Taste	Culinary Art	Benefits	Suitable for
3 Minutes	Spicy	Stir-frying	Appetizing and Helps Digestion	People with Hypertension

• Ingredients

oyster mushrooms 300g, lean pork 100g, red pepper and green pepper, each for 15g, chopped scallion stalk, mashed garlic and ginger as needed

• Seasonings

salt 5g, starchy sauce 10ml, MSG 3g, baking soda 3g, white sugar 3g, cooking wine 3ml, dark soy sauce 3ml, oyster sauce, cooking oil as needed

How to prepare

Step 1

Wash the oyster mushrooms and cut off the roots.

Step 2

Cut the cleaned lean pork into thin slices. Add in some baking soda, salt, MSG to mix well. Add in some cooking oil to preserve for 10 minutes.

Step 3

Add fresh water into a wok and bring to boil, and then add in some cooking oil; add the oyster mushrooms, boil briefly and ladle out.

Step 4

Add in some oil to the wok and heat up to 40% of the oil temperature; Add the sliced pork to stir fry until the flesh turns white, ladle out to use later.

Step 5

Leave some oil in wok, and put in mashed ginger and garlic, chopped scallion stalk, green pepper and red pepper to stir fry to enhance flavor. Add the prepared oyster mushrooms, sliced pork, and add in salt, MSG, white sugar, oyster sauce, dark soy sauce and cooking wine to stir fry for about 1 minute until fully cooked.

Step 6

Dress with starchy sauce, and stir fry evenly. Plate up to finish.

Braised Pork with Chestnuts

Cooking Time	Taste	Culinary Art	Benefits	Suitable for
6 Minutes	Salty	Braising	Lowers Blood Pressure	The Elderly

• Ingredients
pork 500g, chestnuts 70g, sliced ginger, minced garlic, star anise and chopped scallion stalk as needed

• Seasonings
caramel, cooking wine, cooking oil and dark soy sauce needed

Step 1

Wash the pork and cut into small chunks.

Step 2

Heat up the oil in the wok to 40% of the oil temperature, and add the prepared chestnuts to deep fry for 2 minutes to be cooked and scoop it out.

Step 3

Leave some oil in the wok and add the pork to stir fry until the pork fat melts out; add in the cleaned star anise, sliced ginger and minced garlic. Finally, add in caramel to stir fry evenly.

Step 4

Add in cooking wine, dark soy sauce to stir fry fast and evenly, and put in the prepared chestnuts.

Step 5

Add in moderate amounts of fresh water, cover the wok to braise for 2 minutes until it's full of taste.

Step 6

Uncover the wok, and add the chopped scallion stalks to stir fry evenly. Plate up to finish.

CULINARY TIPS

Keep the chestnuts in boiled water, this makes it easier to peel them, and also put the peeled chestnuts in boiled water for a while and stir briefly so that the thin film surrounding the nuts fall off easily.

Braised Pork with Lotus Roots

Cooking Time	Taste	Culinary Art	Benefits	Suitable for
23 Minutes	Salty	Braising	Improve Vitality and Nourish the Blood	Female

• Ingredients
streaky pork 250g, lotus roots 150g, fermented red bean-curd 30g, minced garlic, sliced ginger, shallot sections and the chopped scallion stalk as needed

• Seasonings
white sugar 3g, cooking wine, dark soy sauce, salt, MSG, essence of chicken, starchy sauce and cooking oil as needed

How to prepare

Step 1

Cut the cleaned streaky pork into small chunks and dice the cleaned lotus roots.

Step 2

Add oil to the wok, and put the streaky pork, stir fry until the fat melts away. Add in white sugar and fermented red bean-curd. And add minced garlic, sliced ginger and the shallot. Add the cooking wine to stir fry evenly. Add in dark soy sauce and stir fry to get a richer color.

Step 3

Add in fresh water to the wok, and add lotus root to stir fry evenly. Cover the wok, braise for about 20 minutes until its fully cooked.

Step 4

Uncover the wok, and add in salt, MSG, essence of chicken to stir fry well and season up. Dress with some starchy sauce to stir fry well.

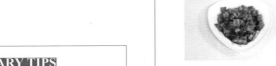

Step 5

Plate up and use some shallot to garnish the dish.

Braised Ribs with Potatoes

Cooking Time	Taste	Culinary Art	Benefits	Suitable for
13 Minutes	Fresh and Delicious	Braising	Reduces Body Bear and Good for Detoxification	General

● Ingredients
potatoes 200g, ribs 500g, green pepper, red pepper 20g each, sliced ginger, mashed garlic, chopped scallion stalk and minced shallot as needed

● Seasonings
salt 4g, essence of chicken 2g, potato starch 2g, cooking wine 5ml, MSG 2g, light soy sauce 3ml, dark soy sauce 3 ml, starchy sauce 10ml and cooking oil as needed

How to prepare

Step 1

Wash the potatoes, peel and cut into small chunks; slice the cleaned red pepper and green pepper.

Step 2

Chop the cleaned ribs in to small chunks and put in a bowl; add in some salt and cooking wine, and then the MSG, light soy sauce to mix well, and finally add the potato starch to mix well.

Step 3

Heat up oil in the wok to 50% of the oil temperature, add in potatoes to deep fry for about 2 minutes, and ladle out the deep fried potatoes to be used later.

Step 5

Leave some oil in wok and add sliced ginger, mashed garlic, chopped scallion stalk to stir fry quickly to enhance the flavor. Add ribs and stir fry evenly. Add cooking wine, and some light soy sauce to stir fry to enhance the flavor, and finally add about 300ml of fresh water, with salt, MSG and essence of chicken.

Step 4

Add ribs and mix well; deep fry until the change of color to ladle out.

Step 6

Add potatoes, and some thick broad-bean sauce to stir fry evenly, and add some dark soy sauce to stir fry evenly. Cover the wok and use a low flame to braise for 10 minutes.

Step 7

Uncover the wok and add the prepared green pepper and red pepper; add in starchy sauce to stir fry evenly until the broth has been dried and reduced into sauce and been full of taste.

Step 8

Plate up and garnish with minced shallot to finish.

CULINARY TIPS

1. Ribs not only contain proteins, fat, vitamins, but also contain plenty of calcium phosphate, ossein, bone glue protein, etc., which can provide calcium for children and the elderly.
2. Add ribs to stir fry in a way that it doesn't get burnt and do not stir fry for too long. This would affect the taste of the finished course.

Steamed Ribs with Plum Sauce

Cooking Time	Taste	Culinary Art	Benefits	Suitable for
20 Minutes	Salty	Steaming	Boost Immunity	Children

• Ingredients
ribs 450g, plum sauce 25g, mashed ginger 15g, minced shallot as needed

• Seasonings
salt, cooking wine, sesame oil, potato starch as needed

How to prepare

Step 1

Wash the ribs and chop into small pieces to put in a dish. Add in minced ginger, salt, cooking wine and mix well. And then pour in the plum sauce and knead well. Cover the ribs with an even layer of potato starch and add a few drops of sesame oil to pickle well.

Step 2

Put the pickled ribs in a dish and arrange them so that there is enough space between them before putting it into the steamer.

Step 3

Cover and steam on a medium flame for 15 minutes until cooked thoroughly.

Step 4

Get the ribs out and garnish with minced shallot to finish.

CULINARY TIPS

Chop the ribs into small chunks and then wash off the blood, which will make the ribs look much whiter after the steaming. After rinsing the ribs, drain off the water and then dress with potato starch, which can make the meat more tender.

• Ingredients
net streaky pork 300g, mashed garlic 30g, chopped scallion, sliced ginger and minced shallot as needed

• Seasonings
salt 3g, cooking wine, MSG, hot chili oil, soy sauce, sesame oil and zanthoxylum oil as needed

How to Prepare

Step 1
Add some fresh water to the wok as needed to heat up, and put in the washed streaky pork, chopped scallion stalk and sliced ginger. Pour some cooking wine for enhancing the flavor. Cover the wok to boil the ingredients with strong flame for 20 minutes until it's fully cooked. Turn off the flame and leave the ingredients in the broth for 20 more minutes.

Step 2
Put the mashed garlic in a bowl, and add salt, MSG, hot chili oil, soy sauce, sesame oil and Sichuan pepper (zanthoxylum) oil as needed. Stir and mix well to be full of taste, and make into the seasoning sauce.

Step 3
Get the boiled streaky pork, and slice into pieces with even thickness to arrange well in a dish.

Step 4
Serve on the prepared sauce and spread on the minced shallot to finish.

CULINARY TIPS
Boil the streaky pork flaccid, turn off the flame to leave the meat soaked in the broth for a while, which will make the meat seasoned well easy.

Cooking Time	Taste	Culinary Art	Benefits	Suitable for
42 Minutes	Spicy	Mixing	Boost Immunity	General

Pork with Garlic Sauce

Braised Pig Feet with Preserved Bean Curd

Cooking Time	Taste	Culinary Art	Benefits	Suitable for
7 Minutes	Salty	Braising	Nourished the Heart and Moistens the Lungs	Male

• Ingredients

pig feet 550g, preserved bean curd 30g, mashed garlic, shallot knots and sliced ginger as needed

• Seasonings

salt, essence of chicken, white sugar, white vinegar, cooking wine, dark soy sauce, starchy sauce and cooking oil as needed

How to prepare

Step 1
Wash the pig feet and chop into small pieces.

Step 2
Add some fresh water to the wok, put in the pig feet and add some white vinegar and mix well.

Step 3
Cover the wok and boil until the food is cooked; ladle out and drain off the water; keep aside to be used later.

Step 4
Heat up some oil in the wok and put in sliced ginger, shallot knots and mashed garlic to stir fry quickly to enhance the flavor. Add in the preserved bean curd to stir fry evenly.

Step 5
Put in the pig feet, add in cooking wine and dark soy sauce to stir fry evenly and color up. Add an appropriate amount of fresh water to boil; add salt and essence of chicken to season.

Step 6
Cover the wok and braise on a medium flame until the food is cooked and fully tender.

Step 7
Uncover the wok, and turn on a strong flame until the broth thicken into a sauce; add in white sugar and stir fry evenly. When the broth has reduced and absorbed by the ingredients, add starch to thicken the sauce.

Step 8
Add cooked hot oil to stir fry evenly. Pick out the shallot knots. Plate up to finish.

Stewed Pig Feet Soup with Peanuts

Cooking Time	Taste	Culinary Art	Benefits	Suitable for
70 Minutes	Plain	Stewing	Beauty and Rejuvenation	Female

• Ingredients
pig feet 500g, lotus root 200g, pre-soaked peanuts 160g, chopped scallion 15g, sliced ginger 10g

• Seasonings
salt, essence of chicken, MSG, chili powder, cooking wine and white vinegar as needed

How to prepare

Step 1

Add an appropriate amount of fresh water to the wok, and then put in the pig feet. Add in some white vinegar and cover the wok to stew until cooked.

Step 2

Ladle out the pig feet and wash for use later.

Step 3

Heat up the wok with hot oil and add the sliced ginger and the chopped scallion to stir fry quickly to enhance the flavor. Add the pig feet pieces and add in some cooking wine to stir fry evenly.

Step 4

Add in enough fresh water, pick out the chopped scallions, and add the peanuts. Put in pieces of lotus root to mix well. Cover the wok and stew for 5 minutes.

Step 5

Transfer the materials to an earthenware pot, use a low flame to stew for 1 hour until the pieces of pig feet are fully cooked and tender.

Step 6

Add salt, essence of chicken, MSG and chili powder to season the stew; mix well to finish.

CULINARY TIPS

When stewing the pig feet, add some vinegar. This would help to dissolve more calcium and phosphorus out of the bone collagen, so as to enhance the nutrition, meanwhile, the dissolved protein can be more easily absorbed by the human body. Secondly, while stewing, the floating greasy foam on the broth should be skimmed off constantly, so that the broth could be cooked well without leaving a greasy taste.

Stir-fried Onion with Streaky Pork

Cooking Time	Taste	Culinary Art	Benefits	Suitable for
5 Minutes	Plain	Stir-frying	Appetizing and Helps Digestion	General

• Ingredients
streaky pork 300g, onion 70g, red pepper 20g, fermented soya beans, mashed garlic, sliced ginger as needed

• Seasonings
salt, dark soy sauce, light soy sauce, MSG, white sugar, cooking wine, starchy sauce as needed

How to Prepare

Step 1

Slice the peeled and cleaned onion. Cut the cleaned red pepper into half from the top, and then into shreds and further into small pieces; cut the cleaned streaky pork into small pieces.

Step 2

Pour some oil in wok to heat up and put in the prepared streaky pork, to stir fry until pork fat melts away; add in dark soy sauce, light soy sauce and stir fry to enhance the flavor.

Step 3

Add the prepared red pepper, onion, as well as fermented soya beans, mashed garlic, sliced ginger to stir fry evenly. Add some cooking wine to the stir-fry.

Step 4

Add in some salt, MSG, white sugar to stir fry to be tasty; dress with starchy sauce and plate up to finish.

BEEF

Chili Beef

Cooking Time	Taste	Culinary Art	Benefits	Suitable for
3 Minutes	Spicy	Stir-frying	Boosts Immunity	Male

• Ingredients
beef 300g, green pepper, red pepper 15g each, chili powder 6g, sliced ginger, mashed garlic and chopped scallion stalk as needed

• Seasonings
cooking oil 30ml, salt 3g, baking soda, light soy sauce, potato starch, MSG, cooking wine, essence of chicken, oyster sauce, dark soy sauce, Sichuan pepper (zanthoxylum) oil, chili oil and starchy sauce as needed

How to prepare

Step 1

Wash the beef and cut into chunks and then into slices. Slice the cleaned red pepper. Cut the cleaned green pepper into small pieces.

Step 2

Add some baking soda, light soy sauce, MSG and salt to the sliced beef and mix well. Also add potato starch and cooking oil and mix well, and marinate the meat for 10 minutes.

Step 3

Add cooking oil to the wok and throw in the prepared green pepper and red pepper and stir well. Ladle out after boiling.

Step 4

Heat up the wok with hot oil until it reaches 50% of the oil temperature Add the sliced beef for a quick fry and then ladle out, when the meat is cooked.

Step 5

Leave some oil in the wok and put sliced ginger, mashed garlic, chopped scallion stalks and chili powder and stir fry quickly to enhance the flavor. Add the prepared green pepper and red pepper and fry evenly. Add the beef and salt, essence of chicken, oyster sauce, dark soy sauce, cooking wine, as well as Sichuan pepper oil and chili oil to stir fry for about 1 minute until cooked.

Step 6

Dress with some starchy sauce, and plate up to finish.

Stir-fried Beef with Snow Peas

Cooking Time	Taste	Culinary Art	Benefits	Suitable for
5 Minutes	Fresh and Delicious	Stir-frying	Boosts Immunity	General

• Ingredients
snow peas 180g, beef 250g, green pepper, red pepper 50g each, sliced ginger, mashed garlic, chopped scallion stalk, 10g each

• Seasonings
salt, MSG, cooking wine, starchy sauce, cooking oil, oyster sauce, white sugar, potato starch and soybean sauce as needed

How to prepare

Step 1

Wash the green and red peppers and remove the core and seeds; cut into pieces. Remove the veins on the snow peas and wash with fresh water; cut off the two ends.

Step 2

Slice the cleaned beef. Add potato starch, soybean sauce, salt and MSG and mix well. Add in starchy sauce and mix well so that it doesn't leave lumps.

Step 3

Add cooking oil to the mixture and let it marinate for a while.

Step 4

Add some hot oil to the wok and heat up; add the pickled beef and stir fry quickly, then scoop it out.

Step 5

Leave some oil in the wok. Add mashed garlic, sliced ginger, and chopped scallion stalk. Add the prepared snow peas and the prepared green pepper and red pepper.

Step 6

Add cooking wine to stir fry evenly. Add the quick-fried beef and put in oyster sauce, salt, MSG, white sugar and stir fry well.

Step 7

Stir fry evenly until fully cooked and plate up to finish.

Stir-fried Beef with Onion

Cooking Time	Taste	Culinary Art	Benefits	Suitable for
2 Minutes	Fresh and Delicious	Stir-frying	Boosts Immunity	General

• Ingredients
beef 300g, onion 100g, sliced red pepper 15g, sliced ginger, mashed garlic and chopped scallion stalks as needed

• Seasonings
salt 3g, MSG and essence of chicken each for 1g, light soy sauce, white sugar, oyster sauce, baking soda, starchy sauce, chili oil and cooking oil as needed

How to prepare

Step 1

Cut the peeled and cleaned onions into several chunks, top-down and then slice it.

Step 3

Boil fresh water; add in beef and scramble it (i.e. break it into chunks) and boil briefly until its just cooked. Ladle out the quick-boiled beef and keep it aside to be used later.

Step 5

Leave some oil in the wok; add in sliced ginger, mashed garlic and chopped scallion stalks to stir fry quickly to enhance the flavor. Add in onions and sliced red pepper to stir fry for about half a minute.

Step 7

Dress with a little starchy sauce. Plate up to finish.

Step 2

Wash the beef clean and cut into slices; add in baking soda, light soy sauce, salt, MSG and stir with chopsticks. Add in starchy sauce and some cooking oil to preserve for 10 minutes to be full of taste.

Step 4

Add oil to the wok and heat up to 50% of the oil temperature, add in beef and scramble it with a ladle. Deep fry quickly for about 1 minute until thoroughly cooked; ladle out for use later.

Step 6

Add beef, salt, MSG, essence of chicken, white sugar, oyster sauce and stir fry evenly. This will add flavor to the beef. Add in chili oil to stir fry well.

Stir-fried Beef with Potatoes

Cooking Time	Taste	Culinary Art	Benefits	Suitable for
4 Minutes	Plain	Stir-frying	Slimming and Expelling of Toxin	General

• Ingredients
potatoes 150g, beef 250g, onion 100g, sliced ginger, mashed garlic, red pepper, chopped scallion stalk as needed

• Seasonings
cooking oil 30ml, salt 3g, baking soda, light soy sauce, MSG, essence of chicken, thick broad-bean sauce, oyster sauce and starchy sauce as needed

How to prepare

Step 1

Peel and clean the potatoes and onions into chunks.

Step 2

Wash the beef and cut into slices, add in baking soda, light soy sauce, MSG and salt and mix well. Add in starchy sauce and some cooking oil, and marinate for 10 minutes.

Step 3

Heat up the fresh water and add in cooking oil and salt to boil up; put in potatoes to cook for about 1 minute until cooked and ladle out for use later.

Step 4

Add beef to mix well, and quickly boil, once the color of the flesh changes ladle out.

Step 5

Heat the oil to 50% of the oil temperature, and add the beef. Quickly fry to ladle out, and then put in sliced ginger, mashed garlic and sliced red pepper and stir fry quickly to enhance the flavor. Add in chopped scallion stalks to stir fry evenly. Put in the prepared onion, sliced potatoes to stir fry well and finally put in the beef.

Step 6

Put in essence of chicken, oyster sauce and thick broad-bean sauce to stir fry evenly so that the dish is full of flavour. Finally add some starchy sauce to thicken the gravy.

Step 7

Add the chopped scallion to stir fry well. Finally, plate up to finish.

The Nourishing Braised Beef Sirloin with Soybean

Cooking Time	Taste	Culinary Art	Benefits	Suitable for
17 Minutes	Fresh and Delicious	Braising	Improve Vitality and Nourish the Blood	General

• Ingredients
pre-soaked soybeans 100g, cooked beef sirloin 200g, red dates 2g, medlar 1g, sliced ginger, mashed garlic, chopped scallion stalks as needed

• Seasonings
salt 2g, white sugar 10g, oyster sauce, five-spice powder, starchy sauce, light soy sauce, cooking wine and cooking oil as needed

Step 1

Wash the beef sirloin and cut into pieces.

Step 2

Heat some oil in the wok. Add sliced ginger, mashed garlic and chopped scallion stalks and stir fry quickly to enhance the flavor. Add the beef sirloin to stir fry well and add in some cooking wine to fry for more flavor; add in a little light soy sauce to stir fry for a deeper color.

Step 3

Add the pre-soaked soybeans and add the cleaned and prepared red dates to stir fry evenly; add in salt, MSG, white sugar and oyster sauce.

Step 4

Add about 200ml of fresh water and stir well. Cover to braise on a low flame for 15 minutes until the beef sirloin and soybeans are both cooked and tender.

Step 5

Uncover the wok and add in medlar and a little five-spice powder to stir fry quickly to enhance the flavor. Use a strong flame to reduce the broth into sauce; finally add starchy sauce to thicken the sauce.

Step 6

Stir fry evenly until the sauce has thickened and is flavorful. Plate up the tender beef sirloin and soybeans.

CULINARY TIPS

The beef sirloin takes a long time to cook until it is tender; therefore, it can be put in a pressure cooker with an appropriate amount of fresh water for steaming. After 30 minutes of cooking on a low flame, the beef sirloin will be fully cooked and tender

Braised Beef Sirloin with Turnips

Cooking Time	Taste	Culinary Art	Benefits	Suitable for
17 Minutes	Salty	Braising	Boosts Immunity	Male

• Materials
cooked beef sirloin 350g, turnips 400g, sectioned garlic bolt 40g, sliced ginger, mashed garlic and chopped scallion stalk as needed

• Seasonings
cooking oil 35ml, salt 17g, cooking wine, essence of chicken, oyster sauce, white sugar, starchy sauce, five-spice powder, sesame oil, Chu Hou Sauce[2] and thick broad-bean sauce as needed

Step 1

Wash and peel the turnips and dice into small pieces; cut the beef sirloin into chunks.

Step 2

Boil up the fresh water and add in salt. Put in turnips and cover the wok to boil for about 5 minutes until cooked.

Step 3

Heat up the oil in a wok, add in sliced ginger, mashed garlic, chopped scallion stalk to stir fry quickly to enhance the flavor. Add in Chu Hou Sauce to stir fry quickly to enhance the flavor, and then add in thick broad-bean sauce to stir fry evenly.

Step 4

Add the beef sirloin to stir fry well. Add in cooking wine to get more flavor and to remove the offensive smell. Add in about 150ml of fresh water to boil up. Add in a little five-spice powder and mix well.

Step 5

Add the turnips to stir fry evenly, and add in salt, essence of chicken, oyster sauce, white sugar and mix well. Cover the wok and use a low flame to stew for several minutes.

Step 6

Add the sectioned garlic cloves and add in a little starchy sauce. Drip in a little sesame oil to stir fry well. Plate up to finish.

2 Chu Hou Sauce: It is one of the traditional special products in Foshan in South China's Guangdong Province. It was first invented by a cook named Leung Chu Hou in the Jiaqing Period of Qing Dynasty, with soybean and wheat flour as ingredients, dried into a paste, and mixed with lard, sugar, sesame, and finalized by double steaming and boiling. It is of a reddish brown color, with the strong flavor and smell of fermented soybeans, very delicious, and is suitable for cooking chicken, duck and fish, etc., especially the Chu Hou Chicken is a very famous dish.

Needle Mushrooms with Beef Rolls

Cooking Time	Taste	Culinary Art	Benefits	Suitable for
10 Minutes	Plain	Steaming	Boost Immunity	Male

• Ingredients
beef 500g, needle mushroom 300g, cilantro 20g, shredded ginger as needed

• Seasonings
cooking oil 30ml, salt 3g, essence of chicken, potato starch, oyster sauce, light soy sauce, white sugar, baking soda and starchy sauce as needed

How to prepare

Step 1

Cut the root of the needle mushroom and put in dish for use later.

Step 2

Wash and slice the beef; add in salt, light soy sauce, essence of chicken, white sugar, baking soda and potato starch to mix well. Add in some cooking oil to preserve for 10 minutes.

Step 3

Add in some water in wok to heat up; add in salt, essence of chicken and oil to boil up; add the needle mushroom, after boiling up to ladle out.

Step 4

Spread the beef flat and put on shredded ginger, cilantro, needle mushroom to roll up and arrange well in dish.

Step 5

Put the beef rolls in steamer to cover, steaming for 7 minutes on a large flame.

Step 6

When the beef roll steamed well, get the beef out to serve up.

Step 7

Heat up the wok with some oil, and then add in 150ml fresh water; Add in salt, essence of chicken, oyster oil and light soy sauce to stir and boil up.

Step 8

Add in some starchy sauce to mix well, which is to make the broth into thick sauce, and then pour it on the beef rolls to finish.

CULINARY TIPS

Preserve the beef in cold water for more than two hours before cooking, to clean off the blood of the flesh, and also to remove the offensive smell of the beef.

Beef in Ginger Sauce

Cooking Time	Taste	Culinary Art	Benefits	Suitable for
2 Minutes	Spicy	Mixing	Boosts Immunity	Children

• Ingredients
spiced beef 100g, minced ginger 15g, chili powder and minced shallots as needed

• Seasonings
salt 3g, light soy sauce 6ml, mature vinegar 7ml, essence of chicken, sesame oil and chili oil as needed

How to prepare

Step 1
Slice the spiced beef and put it in a dish.

Step 2
Get a clean bowl and add minced ginger, chili powder. Put in some minced shallots, and add an appropriate amount of salt, vinegar, essence of chicken; add in some light soy sauce, chili oil and then pour in some sesame oil.

Step 3
Add in some boiled water and mix the seasoning well.

Step 4
Coat the seasoning evenly on the meat to finish.

> **CULINARY TIPS**
> The beef should not be sliced too thick or it won't be seasoned easy.

• Ingredients
cooked pumpkin 300g, beef rolls 200g, red chili pepper "rings" as needed

• Seasonings
salt, MSG, essence of chicken, starchy sauce, cooking wine and cooking oil as needed

How to Prepare

Step 1

Put the cooked pumpkin in a bowl with some fresh water, smash the pumpkin and stir well. Drain the pumpkin juice for later use.

Step 2

Add fresh water into the wok and boil, Add the beef rolls and stir well. Ladle out after boiling.

Step 3

Heat up the wok with some oil, and add the beef rolls; add in cooking wine and stir fry well to enhance the flavor, and then add the pumpkin juice.

Step 4

Add some salt, MSG, essence of chicken to season well. Add some starchy sauce and drip in boiled oil and stir well.

Step 5

Boil for about 1 minute to enhance the taste. Plate up and garnish with some red chili peppers for more flavor.

CULINARY TIPS

When boiling the beef rolls, you should control the intensity of the flame and the heat of oil, don't boil the beef rolls for too long, in case the beef rolls turn tough. This could affect its taste..

Cooking Time	Taste	Culinary Art	Benefits	Suitable for
3 Minutes	Fresh and Delicious	Boiling	Nourishes the Heart and Moistens the Lungs	Female

Golden Soup of Beef Rolls

Turnip Soup with Beef Balls

Cooking Time	Taste	Culinary Art	Benefits	Suitable for
6 Minutes	Fresh and Delicious	Boiling	Improves Appetite and Helps Digestion	The Elderly

• Ingredients
turnip 150g, beef balls 100g, sliced ginger and minced shallot as needed

• Seasonings
salt 3g, essence of chicken 2g, MSG, cooking wine and cooking oil as needed

How to Prepare

Step 1

Do the criss-cross cutting on the washed beef balls and cut the washed turnips into slices.

Step 2

Heat up some oil in the wok, and add the sliced ginger to stir fry to enhance the flavor, pour in a little cooking wine, and add in some fresh water. Turn on a strong flame and add the turnips. Cover to boil for a while.

Step 3

Uncover the wok and put in the beef balls. Cover and switch to a medium flame and boil until the ingredients are fully cooked. Add in salt, MSG and essence of chicken to season well. Stir well so that the dish is full of flavor.

Step 4

Ladle out the soup into a bowl and garnish with some minced shallot to finish.

CULINARY TIPS

Beef balls have a high nutritive value, and are abundant in protein, fat, vitamin B and calcium, phosphorus, iron, as well as other elements, that can help invigorate the spleen and stomach and replenish your "Qi" (i.e. Improve Vitality), as well as strengthening the tendons & bones. Eating beef balls can also promote the disease resistance capacity of the body, which is especially essential for people after surgery when they are recovering.

MUTTON

Spicy Mutton with Beer

Cooking Time	Taste	Culinary Art	Benefits	Suitable for
45 Minutes	Spicy	Braising	Protects The Liver And Kidneys	Male

• Ingredients
mutton 500g, chopped dried chili 25g, beer 200g, sliced ginger, chopped garlic cloves as needed

• Seasonings
salt, oyster sauce, chili sauce, chili oil, starchy sauce and cooking oil as needed.

How to prepare

Step 1

Wash the mutton and chop into pieces. Add some water into the wok and put mutton. Quickly boil for a while to remove the offensive smell, and then ladle out to put on a dish for later use.

Step 2

Heat up some oil in the wok and put in sliced ginger to stir fry briefly. Put in mutton and stir fry evenly. Add the cleaned chopped dried chili to stir fry evenly. Add in some beer and then some salt, oyster sauce and chili sauce and stir fry well.

Step 3

Cover to braise for 40 minutes until the mutton is tender.

Step 4

Uncover the wok and add in some chopped garlic cloves. And then put in some chopped garlic sprout leaves and chili oil and stir fry well. Add in starchy sauce and stir fry quickly.

Step 5

Pour the ingredients in the wok to a clay pot to simmer for a while. Turn off the flame and serve the clay pot with mutton.

CULINARY TIPS

The rotten ginger could produce a very poisonous substance which can cause the degeneration and necrosis of the liver cells, and also can cause all kinds of symptoms of cancer; therefore, rotten ginger should not be used.

Mutton Steamed with Rice Flour

Cooking Time	Taste	Culinary Art	Benefits	Suitable for
32 Minutes	Plain	Steaming	Boosts Immunity	General

• Ingredients
mutton 300g, rice flour for steaming meat 50g, minced garlic, ginger, red pepper and shallot as needed

• Seasonings
cooking wine, light soy sauce, salt, MSG, essence of chicken and cooking oil as needed

How to prepare

Step 1

Wash the mutton and cut the mutton fat into thick shreds; the cleaned lean mutton should be cut into thin slices. Add in cooking wine, light soy sauce, salt, MSG, essence of chicken and mix well.

Step 2

sprinkle rice flour and knead well. And then add in mashed red pepper, ginger and garlic and knead well.

Step 3

Lay the shredded mutton fat on a dish, and then the lean mutton slices.

Step 4

Put the dish into a steamer, and cover to steam for 30 minutes until it is cooked.

Step 5

Take out the dish of mutton; add some oil in the wok and heat up, and then pour the hot oil on the mutton.

Step 6

garnish with minced shallot to finish.

Lamb Chops with Potatoes

Cooking Time	Taste	Culinary Art	Benefits	Suitable for
7 Minutes	Fresh and Delicious	Braising	Protects The Liver And Kidneys	Male

• Ingredients

stewed lamb chop 450g, potatoes 250g, a little sliced carrots, chopped garlic bolts 25g, sliced ginger 10g

• Seasonings

salt 3g, cooking wine, MSG, white sugar, oyster oil, cooking oil, starchy sauce and scallion oil as needed

How to prepare

Step 1

Chop the stewed lamb into sections; peel and wash the potatoes and cut into pieces.

Step 2

Heat some oil in the wok and put in ginger and stir fry quickly to enhance the flavor. Add the prepared potatoes and lamb chops to stir fry evenly. Add in some cooking wine as needed.

Step 3

Add in some fresh water. Cover the wok and braise on a large flame for 10 minutes until fully cooked and tender.

Step 4

Uncover the wok, add in salt, MSG, white sugar and oyster sauce and stir fry evenly. Put in sliced carrots and some chopped garlic cloves and stir fry well.

Step 5

Add in some starchy sauce and mix well, and then add in scallion oil and some chopped garlic sprout leaves to stir fry briefly until cooked.

Step 6

Pour the cooked items in the wok into a heated clay pot, to simmer for a while. Turn off the flame and serve the clay pot with lamb chops.

CULINARY TIPS

The peeled potatoes if not cooked immediately, should be kept in cool water, otherwise it turns a dark color, however, it can not be immersed for too long, then the nutrition is lost.

Stewed Mutton Tenderloin with Turnip

Cooking Time	Taste	Culinary Art	Benefits	Suitable for
45 Minutes	Plain	Boiling	Provides Protection Against Cancer	General

• Ingredients
turnips 300g, tenderloin mutton 200g, cilantro and sliced ginger as needed

• Seasonings
salt, essence of chicken, chili powder, cooking wine as needed

How to prepare

Step 1

Wash the turnips and cut into thin slices.

Step 2

Add water to the wok to boil up and put the mutton tenderloin for a quick-boil, and ladle out to drain off water and keep aside to use later.

Step 3

Wash the wok, add fresh water again and boil up; put in sliced ginger and the turnips; and then add the mutton tenderloin; add a little cooking wine and mix well. Cover the wok to boil.

Step 4

Move the materials in the wok to a clay pot. Put on a low flame and cover to boil for 40 minutes..

Step 5

Uncover the clay pot, and add salt, essence of chicken to stir until the dish is full of flavor. Turn off the flame and serve the clay pot.

Step 6

Garnish with cleaned cilantro, and sprinkle a little chili powder to finish.

CULINARY TIPS

Turnips have less calories while they are rich in cellulose. Eating more turnips will make people feel full easily after dining; therefore, it is helpful to losing weight. In addition to this, turnips contain plenty of Vitamin A and Vitamin C, which are essential elements to boost immunity, have stronger cells and enhance the body's ability to fight cancer.

Stewed Mutton in Soup-stock

Cooking Time	Taste	Culinary Art	Benefits	Suitable for
8 Minutes	Plain	Boiling	Beauty and Rejuvenation	Female

• Ingredients
mutton 350g, Chinese cabbage 150g, turnips, bell pepper and sliced ginger as needed, thick soup 1000ml.

• Seasonings
salt, MSG, essence of chicken, cooking wine, cooking oil, starchy sauce as needed.

How to prepare

Step 1

Wash the mutton and cut into slices. Cut the Chinese cabbage into slices, as well as the turnips. Wash the color peppers and cut into slices.

Step 2

Add some cooking wine, essence of chicken, salt and MSG to the mutton and knead them well, and then dress it with starchy sauce and let it marinate for 10 minutes to soak up the flavours.

Step 3

Heat some oil in the wok and put sliced ginger, and then the Chinese cabbage and turnips to stir fry well.

Step 4

Add in some water to stir fry well, and then the broth, boil on a strong flame. Add in salt, MSG, essence of chicken and finally add the sliced color peppers to mix well.

Step 5

Add the marinated mutton, after stirring (not mixing) well let it boil for 3 minutes until it's fully cooked and tender.

Step 6

Turn off the flame and plate up to finish.

CULINARY TIPS

The Chinese cabbage can be put into boiling water for a quick boil, which will not only reduce the cooking time of the vegetables, but also will prevent oxidation, so as to retain vitamin C.

Spicy Lamb Chops

Cooking Time	Taste	Culinary Art	Benefits	Suitable for
6 Minutes	Spicy	Stir-frying	Protects the Liver and Kidneys	General

• Ingredients

stewed lamb chop 500g, minced red chili peppers 40g, cooked white sesame seed 3g, sliced ginger and chopped scallion stalks, 10g each, Sichuan pepper 15g.

• Seasonings

salt, MSG, light soy sauce, potato starch, cooking wine, chili oil, Sichuan pepper (zanthoxylum) oil and cooking oil as needed

How to Prepare

Step 1

Wash the lamb chop clean and cut into chunks, and put in a bowl. Add in some light soy sauce and potato starch, knead and mix with the hand, and then let it marinate for 10 minutes So that it is more flavorful.

Step 2

Add enough oil to the wok and put in the lamb chops to deep-fry for about 1 to 2 minutes until the surface turns into a golden color, ladle out onto a dish.

Step 3

Leave some oil in the wok; add in the chopped scallion stalks and sliced ginger, and then put in Sichuan pepper and red chili peppers to stir fry quickly to enhance the flavor. Add the lamb chops to stir fry for about 3 minutes until it is fully cooked. Add in salt, MSG and cooking wine.

Step 4

Add in chili oil and Sichuan pepper oil to stir fry evenly. Spread on some chopped shallot to stir fry evenly and plate up. Garnish with some cooked white sesame seed to finish.

CULINARY TIPS

When deep-frying the lamb chops, the heat should be controlled at 40% to 60% of the oil temperature, with a low flame, otherwise, the surface of the lame chops will easily become over-fried or get burnt dark, both of which will affect the taste.

POULTRY
MEAT &

Steamed Eggs with Three Delicacies

Cooking Time	Taste	Culinary Art	Benefits	Suitable for
9 Minutes	Plain	Steaming	Clears the Heat and Good for Detoxification	Pregnant and Lactating Mothers

• Ingredients

2 eggs, shrimp meat 30g, carrots 35g, peas 30g

• Seasonings

salt 4g, starchy sauce 10ml, MSG 3g, essence of chicken 6g, chili powder, sesame oil and cooking oil as needed

How to prepare

Step 1

Peel the carrots and cut into thick slices and then cut into strips, and dice it further.

Step 2

Wash the shrimps and cut into halves from the back and then dice it. Add some salt, MSG, and then add some starchy sauce and mix well. let it marinate for 5 minutes.

Step 3

Boil fresh water in a wok, add some salt, and then add the diced carrot, and add some cooking oil. Add the cleaned peas and mix well. Cook for about 1 minute. Add shrimp meat and cook for another minute. Ladle out the ingredients into a bowl for later use.

Step 4

Crack the eggs into a bowl and add salt, chili powder and essence of chicken and beat the eggs. Add in a little warm water and mix well and then add in some sesame oil.

Step 5

Put a bowl in the steamer and add the prepared egg mixture. Cover the steamer and steam on a low flame for about 7 minutes.

Step 6

Uncover the steamer and put in the prepared ingredients (see step 3).

Step 7

Cover and steam for 2 minutes until its fully cooked.

Step 8

Take the steamed egg and let it cool for a while before dining.

Fried Chicken Shreds in Assorted Colors

Cooking Time	Taste	Culinary Art	Benefits	Suitable for
2 Minutes	Spicy	Stir-frying	Appetizing and Help Digestion	General

• Ingredients

chicken breast 200g, pre-soaked black forest mushrooms 35g, green peppers and red peppers each for 20g, carrots and potatoes each for 20g, minced garlic and shredded ginger as needed

• Seasonings

salt 6g, MSG 1g, starchy sauce 10ml, cooking wine and cooking oil as needed

How to prepare

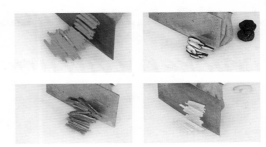

Step 1

Peel and wash the carrots to cut into slices, and then into shreds. Cut the pre-soaked black forest mushrooms into shreds. Wash the green peppers and red peppers and cut into shreds. Peel and wash the potatoes and cut into slices and then into shreds.

Step 2

Wash the chicken breast to cut into slices and then into shreds. Add some salt, MSG and starchy sauce and mix well. Drip in some cooking oil and let it marinate for 10 minutes.

Step 3

Boil fresh water in a wok; add in salt and some cooking oil and stir well. Add prepared carrots, potatoes, black forest mushrooms, green peppers and red peppers and stir well. Ladle out the cooked ingredients to use later.

Step 4

Add the chicken shreds and scramble it, and quickly boil until the color changes and ladle out.

Step 5

Heat up the wok with oil and put in shredded ginger and minced garlic to stir fry quickly to enhance the flavor. Add the prepared carrots, potatoes, black forest mushrooms, green peppers and red peppers, and then the shredded chicken and stir fry well.

Step 6

Add salt, MSG and cooking wine to the stir-fry. Add in some starchy sauce and mix evenly. Plate up to finish.

CULINARY TIPS

Add some chili oil or chili paste during the stir-frying will bring an even better taste.

Kung Pao Chicken (spicy diced chicken with peanuts)

Cooking Time	Taste	Culinary Art	Benefits	Suitable for
4 Minutes	Spicy	Stir-frying	Boost Immunity	General

• Ingredients
chicken breast 300g, cucumber 80g, peanuts 50g, dried chili 7g, garlic 10g, sliced ginger as needed

• Seasonings
salt 5g, MSG 2g, essence of chicken 3g, cooking wine 3ml, potato starch, cooking oil, chili oil and sesame oil as needed

How to prepare

Step 1

Cut the chicken breast into slices with 1cm thickness, and then into strips. Then dice it into cubes. Dice the cucumber the same way and make sure the cubes are the same size as the cubes of chicken. Wash the garlic and dice it.

Step 2

Add some salt, MSG and cooking wine to the diced chicken and mix well. Add in potato starch and coat the chicken evenly. Add some cooking oil to the mixture and let it marinate for 10 minutes.

Step 3

Boil some fresh water. Add peanuts to cook for about 1 minute; ladle out the peanuts and drain off the water.

Step 4

Add some oil to the wok and to heat up to 60% of the oil temperature; deep-fry the peanuts for about 2 minutes. Ladle out the well fried peanuts.

Step 7

Add in some chili oil. Add in some sesame oil and keep on stir-frying for a while.

Step 5

Put in the chicken dices to scramble up and deep fry until the color changes and ladle out.

Step 6

Heat up some oil in the wok and add the diced garlic and sliced ginger to stir fry quickly to enhance the flavor. And then add the dried chili to stir fry to make it more delicious. Add in the prepared cucumber to stir fry well, and then the salt, MSG and essence of chicken to stir fry well. Finally, add the chicken dices to the stir-fry.

Step 8

Plate up and garnish with the fried peanuts to finish.

Braised Sanhuang Chicken with Pickled Chili

Cooking Time	Taste	Culinary Art	Benefits	Suitable for
4 Minutes	Spicy	Braising	Improve Vitality and Nourish the Blood	Female

• Ingredients
Sanhuang Chicken[3] 300g, pickled bell peppers 20g, lettuce 100g, sliced ginger, mashed garlic and chopped scallion stalks as needed

• Seasonings
salt 6g, essence of chicken 4g, MSG 1g, light soy sauce 5ml, potato starch, cooking wine, starchy sauce and cooking oil as needed

CULINARY TIPS

When stir frying the chunks of chicken, add some red chili oil to make it more delicious.

3　Sanhuang Chicken: the Sanhuang Chicken dish was given its name by Zhu Yuanzhang, the initial emperor of Ming Dynasty. The key features of this dish are the tender flesh, fresh taste and its full of nutritions. It is both popular home and abroad. It gets its name of Sanhuang Chicken.

How to prepare

Step 1

Wash the lettuce and roll-cut it into pieces.

Step 2

Wash the chicken meat and cut it into chunks. Add in some essence of chicken, salt, light soy sauce and cooking wine to mix well. Add in some starchy sauce and mix well and let it marinate for 10 minutes to add flavor.

Step 3

Add some oil in the wok to heat up to 50% of the oil temperature; add the chunks of chicken and stir fry until the color changes and ladle out for later use.

Step 4

Leave some oil in the wok, add in sliced ginger, mashed garlic, chopped scallion stalks to stir fry quickly to enhance the flavor. Put in the prepared lettuce and pickled bell peppers to stir fry for a while.

Step 5

Add the stir-fried chicken chunks, and then drip in some cooking wine to the stir-fry.

Step 6

Add about 100ml of fresh water. Add salt, MSG, light soy sauce and essence of chicken and stir fry evenly.

Step 7

Cover the wok and braise on a low flame for 2 minutes until it's fully cooked.

Step 8

Uncover the wok and add some starchy sauce, reduce the broth into a sauce, and finally plate up to finish.

Simmered Chicken with Chestnuts

Cooking Time	Taste	Culinary Art	Benefits	Suitable for
8 Minutes	Salty	Simmering	Lowers Blood Pressure	The Elderly

• Ingredients

Chicken 200g, chestnuts 80g, fresh black forest mushrooms 20g, mashed garlic, sliced ginger, chopped scallion stalk and chopped garlic as needed

• Seasonings

cooking oil, dark soy sauce, salt, MSG, white sugar, light soy sauce, starchy sauce, cooking wine and potato starch as needed.

How to prepare

Step 1

Wash the chicken meat and chop into chunks. Cut the prepared chestnuts in half. Wash the fresh black forest mushroom and cut into shreds.

Step 2

Add some cooking wine, light soy sauce, salt and potato starch to the chicken and mix well.

Step 3

Add some oil in to a wok to heat up to 50% of the oil temperature; add the chestnuts to stir fry quickly and ladle out.

Step 4

Add the chicken chunks to stir fry quickly for about 3 minutes until it's cooked, and scoop out for later use.

Step 5

Leave some oil in the wok, add in chopped scallion stalk, sliced ginger and mashed garlic, and then put in the prepared black forest mushrooms and chicken, with some cooking wine and stir fry well. Add in some dark soy sauce to stir fry well.

Step 6

Add the chestnuts. Add in some fresh water and boil for 4 minutes, and then add in salt, MSG, white sugar and light soy sauce.

Step 7

Add in some starchy sauce, and the chopped garlic.

Step 8

Put in a dry pot to finish.

Stewed Rural Chicken Soup with Chestnuts

Cooking Time	Taste	Culinary Art	Benefits	Suitable for
65 Minutes	Fresh and Delicious	Stewing	Improve Vitality and Nourish the Blood	Female

• Ingredients
rural chicken/ free-range chicken 300g, chestnuts 80g, carrots, sliced ginger and chopped scallion stalk as needed

• Seasonings
salt, white sugar, cooking wine and chili powder as needed

How to prepare

Step 1

Wash the chicken and cut into chunks; peel and wash the carrots, and slice them.

Step 2

Add enough fresh water to the wok and heat it before putting the chicken chunks. Quickly boil for about 3 minutes until it is just cooked; use a slotted ladle to ladle out and drain off the water and keep the chicken for later use.

Step 3

Add fresh water to a wok; add the boiled chicken chunks and add in sliced ginger. Put in the cleaned chestnuts. Cover the wok to boil up and stew on a low flame for about 1 hour until it is fully cooked and tender.

Step 4

Uncover the wok and add salt, white sugar and cooking wine. Put the sliced carrots. sprinkle some chili powder, and chopped scallion and stir well.

Step 5

Finish the stewing, and ladle the soup into a bowl to enjoy.

CULINARY TIPS

When stewing, the salt should not be added too early. This will mak the protein of chicken to coagulate and then the chicken meat becomes hard and tight, which will affect the amount of nutrients that dissolve into the broth. Furthermore, the stewed chicken will be tough and hard to chew.

Stewed Rural Chicken with Ginkgo Nuts

Cooking Time	Taste	Culinary Art	Benefits	Suitable for
125 Minutes	Plain	Stewing	Nourishing Heart and Moistening Lungs	The Elderly

• Ingredients

a whole prepared chicken, pork bones 450g, lean pork 100g, ginkgo nuts 120g, shallot and cilantro 15g each, ginger 20g and medlar 10g.

• Seasonings

salt 4g, chili powder a bit as needed

How to prepare

Step 1

Wash the lean pork and cut into pieces; pat the ginger crushed.

Step 2

Add water to the wok and put in the pork bones, chicken meat and lean pork, cover to boil up on a large flame; uncover the wok and ladle out for later use.

Step 3

Put an earthenware cooking pot on a strong flame; add an appropriate amount of water, add ginger and shallot, and then add the pork bones, chicken meat, lean pork and ginkgo nuts. Cover and boil; switch to asmall flame and let it stew for 2 hours.

Step 4

Uncover the earthenware cooking pot to add salt, chili powder, and then some medlar to give it a better look. Pick off the ginger and shallot. Garnish with cilantro to finish.

CULINARY TIPS

After peeling off the shell of the ginkgo nuts, put them in hot water for a quick boil. This will help to remove the film of the nuts. When stewing the chicken soup, add some black forest mushrooms according to one's own taste. However, don't add too much, so as to preserve the original taste of the chicken soup.

Steamed Chicken with Pumpkin

Cooking Time	Taste	Culinary Art	Benefits	Suitable for
16 Minutes	Sweet	Steaming	Anti-hypertension and Anti-diabetics	The Elderly

• Ingredients
pumpkin 300g, chicken 500g, sliced ginger, chopped scallion stalk and minced shallot as needed

• Seasonings
salt 3g, white sugar 2g, cooking wine, light soy sauce, oyster sauce, essence of chicken, potato starch and cooking oil as needed

How to prepare

Step 1

Peel and wash the pumpkin and cut into small cubes.

Step 2

Wash the chicken and cut into small chunks. Put in a bowl and add in the chopped scallion stalks and sliced ginger. Add some light soy sauce, salt, essence of chicken, oyster sauce, white sugar and cooking wine and mix well. Add an appropriate amount of potato starch to stir well. And then drip in some cooking oil and let it marinate for 10 minutes.

Step 3

Put the prepared pumpkin in a dish and place the marinated chicken chunks on them.

Step 4

Put the dish of chicken and pumpkin in a steamer. Cover and steam on a medium flame for 15 minutes until its fully cooked and tender.

Step 5

Uncover the steamer and take out the chicken chunks and pumpkin, and garnish with minced shallot to finish.

CULINARY TIPS

The washed chicken chunks should be drained off water and then marinated to add flavor. While steaming the food, the flame should be controlled well; if the flame is too strong, the chicken tends to be over-steamed and tough.

Cola Chicken Wings

Cooking Time	Taste	Culinary Art	Benefits	Suitable for
8 Minutes	Fresh and Delicious	Simmering	Improves Vitality and Nourishes the Blood	Female

• Ingredients
chicken wings 300g, sliced ginger and chopped scallion as needed

• Seasonings
light soy sauce 8ml, white sugar 1g, cooking wine 7ml, cola 200ml, dark soy sauce 2ml, cooking oil as needed

Step 1

Put the chicken wings in a bowl and add in light soy sauce, white sugar and cooking wine. Add in chopped scallion and ginger to mix well. Pickle for 15 minutes.

Step 2

Heat up the wok with hot oil until it reaches 50% of the oil temperature, put in the chicken wings to stir and deep-fry for about 2 minutes, until the surface of the chicken wings turn golden, then ladle out.

Step 3

Leave some oil in the wok, put in sliced ginger and chopped scallion to stir fry quickly to enhance flavor. Add chicken wings and add in cooking wine to the stir-fry to enhance flavour.

Step 4

Add in 200ml of cola to mix well, and use a low flame and cover to braise for 5 minutes.

Step 5

Uncover the wok cook on a strong flame, add some dark soy sauce and let the broth thicken.

Step 6

Plate up the stir fried chicken wings.

Simmered Chicken Wings

Cooking Time	Taste	Culinary Art	Benefits	Suitable for
4 Minutes	Plain	Simmering	Improves Vitality and Nourishes the Blood	Female

• Ingredients
chicken wings 500g, wine 100g, sliced ginger and shallot as needed

• Seasonings
salt 5g, light soy sauce, white sugar, MSG, cooking wine, cooking oil and Sichuan pepper (zanthoxylum) oil

CULINARY TIPS
The chicken wings must be drained well to remove all the moisture, or it will create oil splashes when deep-frying. In addition, the flame should be controlled well when deep frying the chicken wings, if not they will be over fried and their color will be too dark.

How to prepare

Step 1

Wash the chicken wings and do the crisscross cutting on them; peel and wash the potatoes and cut into small chunks.

Step 2

Add the chicken wings with salt, cooking wine and caramel to knead well and let it marinate for a while.

Step 3

Heat up some oil in the wok up to 50% of the oil temperature. Add the chicken wings to fry briefly before taking it out and draining off the oil.

Step 4

Add the potatoes chunks and deep fry until cooked; ladle out and drain off the oil.

Step 5

Leave some oil and add in chopped dried chili, sliced ginger and chopped scallion and stir fry quickly to enhance the flavor. Add thick broad-bean sauce and stir fry well.

Step 6

Add in some fresh water, and put in the chicken wings and potatoes to stir fry well.

Step 7

Cover the wok and braise for about 1 minute until it's cooked.

Step 8

Uncover the wok; add in salt and white sugar to cook for a while. Add in oyster sauce and stir fry well. Mix starchy sauce, and a few drops of chili oil to the stir-fry.

Step 9

Add in some Sichuan pepper (zanthoxylum) oil and stir fry evenly, and sprinkle some chopped scallion.

Step 10

Plate up to finish.

Stewed Chicken with Mushrooms

Cooking Time	Taste	Culinary Art	Benefits	Suitable for
5 Minutes	Fresh and Delicious	Stewing	Improve Vitality and Nourish the Blood	Female

• Ingredients
pre-soaked sweet potato vermicelli 120g, mushrooms 100g, cooked chicken meat 400g, chopped scallion 20g, sliced garlic, red peppers and ginger each for 10g, star anise, cassia bark and dried chili as needed, some Thirteen-Spice[4].

• Seasonings
salt 4g, starchy sauce 10ml, oyster sauce, cooking wine, dark soy sauce, MSG, essence of chicken, white sugar and cooking oil as needed.

4 Thirteen kinds of spices are powdered together.

How to prepare

Step 1

Chop the cooked chicken into pieces; and cut the pre-soaked sweet potato vermicelli into sections.

Step 2

Boil the fresh water and add the sweet potato vermicelli for quick-boiling until turning soft. Ladle out to get in a bowl.

Step 3

Add the washed and cut mushrooms to scramble up; after quick-boiling to be cooked, ladle out and get in a bowl.

Step 4

Heat some oil in the wok and Add chicken pieces; after stir frying quickly for a while to scoop out.

Step 5

Leave some oil in the wok and add in dried chili, star anise and cassia bark to stir fry quickly to enhance the flavor. Add the sliced ginger and garlic to stir fry evenly. Put in the boiled mushrooms and then the chicken meat; add cooking wine, dark soy sauce, oyster sauce, salt, MSG, white sugar and essence of chicken, to stir fry for half a minute before further seasoning.

Step 6

Add sweet potato vermicelli to stir fry well, and then add in some Thirteen-Spice to stir fry well. Add the red pepper, to stew for a while and dress with some starchy sauce.

Step 7

Add the chopped scallion, to stir fry to be fully cooked; plate upto finish.

Sliced Chicken with Sesame

Cooking Time	Taste	Culinary Art	Benefits	Suitable for
3 Minutes	Fresh and Delicious	Deep Frying	Boost Immunity	General

• Ingredients
chicken breast 300g, sesame and beaten egg liquid as needed

• Seasonings
salt, MSG, cooking wine and potato starch as needed

How to prepare

Step 1

Wash the chicken breast and pat flaccid and loose with the spine of a chopping knife; add in salt, MSG and cooking wine to mix well.

Step 2

Add the chicken slices with beaten eggs liquid to mix well, and spread on potato starch to stir well. Dress with sesame and put on a dish for use later.

Step 3

Heat some oil in the wok to 50% of the oil temperature; add the chicken slices for deep frying with low flame for about 2 minutes until cooked and ladle out. Drain off the chicken to put on a dish.

Step 4

Cut the chicken slices further into small chunks and arrange well on a dish to finish.

CULINARY TIPS

During the deep frying of chicken slices, control the flame and the temperature of the oill; if the chicken slices are thin, they should not be fried for long, which will affect the taste.

• Ingredients

duck 350g, pod peppers 25g, dried chili 10g, sliced ginger and chopped scallion as needed

• Seasonings

salt, cooking wine, MSG, oyster sauce, starchy sauce, chili paste, chili oil and cooking oil as needed

How to Prepare

Step 1

Wash the duck clean and chop into dices; wash the pod pepper and chop into "rings".

Step 2

Heat some oil in the wok and put in duck dices to stir fry delicious; add cooking wine, salt, MSG, oyster sauce to stir fry for about 2 minutes to be cooked.

Step 3

Drip in some fresh water and add chili paste to stir fry well. And then add sliced ginger, chopped scallion stalk, pod pepper and dried chili to stir fry quickly to enhance the flavor.

Step 4

Dress with starchy sauce and drip in some chili oil to stir fry evenly and plate up to finish.

CULINARY TIPS

During the pickling of duck, add some white spirit, which makes easier to remove the offensive smell of the duck.

Cooking Time	Taste	Culinary Art	Benefits	Suitable for
5 Minutes	Spicy	Stir-frying	Appetizing and Help Digestion	Male

Stir-fried Diced Duck with Chili

Simmered Duck with Potatoes

Cooking Time	Taste	Culinary Art	Benefits	Suitable for
15 Minutes	Salty	Simmering	Appetizing and Help Digestion	The Elderly

• Ingredients
potatoes 250g, duck meat 350g, sliced ginger 25g, mashed garlic 25g, chopped scallion 25g

• Seasonings
cooking wine 5ml, oyster sauce 4g, dark soy sauce 3ml, starchy sauce 8ml and cooking oil as needed

How to prepare

Step 1

Peel, wash and cut the potatoes into chunks; wash the duck and cut into chunks as well.

Step 2

Heat some oil in the wok until 40% to 50% of the oil temperature; Add the potatoes to deep-fry for about 4 minutes to be cooked; ladle out and drain off for use later.

Step 3

Leave some oil in the wok and put in the duck chunks to stir fry for 2 minutes. Add sliced ginger, chopped scallion and mashed garlic. Add cooking wine, oyster sauce and dark soy sauce.

Step 4

Add some fresh water and cover the wok to simmer for about 8 minutes until cooked.

Step 5

Add the fried potatoes to simmer for a while. Dress with starchy sauce and drip in boiled oil.

Step 6

Stir fry for a while to be tasty. Spread on some chopped scallion before plating up.

CULINARY TIPS

After peeling the potatoes, keep them in water and drip in some vinegar, so that the potatoes won't turn dark.

Stewed Duck Soup with Turnips and Bamboo Fungus

Cooking Time	Taste	Culinary Art	Benefits	Suitable for
50 Minutes	Plain	Stewing	Lowering Blood Lipid	Patients with High Blood Lipids

• Ingredients
duck 500g, turnips 300g, pre-soaked bamboo fungus 30g, shallots knot and sliced ginger as needed

• Seasonings
salt 3g, MSG, essence of chicken, chili powder and cooking wine as needed

How to prepare

Step 1

Peel and wash the turnips and cut into chunks; pinch off the root of the bamboo fungus. Chop the washed duck into chunks.

Step 2

Add fresh water into the wok and bring to boil and add duck chunks for quick-boiling of about 2 minutes to be cooked and ladle out.

Step 3

Heat some oil in the wok and put in the cleaned shallots knots and sliced ginger to stir fry quickly to enhance the flavor. Add duck chunks to stir fry well. Drip in cooking wine to stir fry to be more delicious.

Step 4

Add enough fresh water and cover to boil.

Step 6

Cover the pot and turn to strong flame to boil, and then use a low flame to stew for 40 minutes until the duck is fully flaccid and tender.

Step 5

Uncover the wok and add turnips and bamboo fungus to boil. Transfer the turnips, duck chunks, bamboo fungus and soup thoroughly into an earthenware pot.

Step 7

Uncover the wok and skim off the unwanted greases on surface, and then skim off the unwanted greases on surface; add salt, MSG, essence of chicken and chili powder for seasoning.

Step 8

Plate up to finish.

Simmered Young Pigeons

Cooking Time	Taste	Culinary Art	Benefits	Suitable for
10 Minutes	Fresh and Delicious	Simmering	Refreshing and Brain Fitness	General

• Ingredients
flesh of young pigeon 300g, sectioned garlic bolt and pre-soaked black forest mushroom each for 30g, sliced garlic and ginger each for 20g; green and red pepper rings each for 20g

• Seasonings
oyster sauce, salt, MSG, white sugar, dark soy sauce, starchy sauce, light soy sauce, cooking oil, cooking wine and potato starch as needed

How to prepare

Step 1
Chop the washed pigeon flesh in chunks and put in a bowl; add light soy sauce, salt, MSG, cooking wine and starchy sauce to mix well for pickling.

Step 2
Heat some oil in the wok until 30% to 40% of the oil temperature; put in sliced garlic for deep frying until turning golden to ladle out.

Step 3
Leave some oil in the wok to add the pigeon flesh. Deep fry to be cooked and ladle out.

Step 4
Leave some oil in the wok, add the sliced garlic, black forest mushrooms and sliced ginger. And then add the fried pigeon meat, and add cooking wine to mix well.

Step 5
Add some fresh water, and then the oyster sauce, salt, MSG, white sugar and dark soy sauce to stir well.

Step 6
Add green pepper and red pepper rings, and then the sectioned garlic bolt; add in some starchy sauce and stir fry well.

Step 7
Transfer the stir-fried pigeon into an earthenware pot, and put on flame. Cover and simmer with medium flame.

Step 8
Turn off the flame; get the earthenware pot from the flame.

CULINARY TIPS

Before cooking the pigeon flesh, it can be put in boiling water to clean off the blood stain first, so that the simmered pigeon meat can have the genuine cuisine color and taste.

Rabbit Meat Mixed with Celery

Cooking Time	Taste	Culinary Art	Benefits	Suitable for
2.5 Minutes	Fresh and Delicious	Mixing	Appetizing and Help Digestion	General

• Ingredients
cooked rabbit meat 500g, celery 100g, red pepper 20g, mashed garlic as needed

• Seasonings
salt 3g, light soy sauce 3ml, essence of chicken, chili oil, sesame oil and cooking oil as needed

How to prepare

Step 1

Wash the celery and cut into sections with 3cm long. Wash the red pepper and cut into half from the top and remove the seeds, and finally cut into shreds.

Step 2

Remove the bones of the rabbit, and then cut the flesh into shreds.

Step 3

Add an appropriate amount of fresh water into the wok and bring to boil and then add some cooking oil, salt, and add the celery and shreds of red peppers, to boil for about 1 minute to be cooked.

Step 4

Ladle the cooked celery and shreds of red peppers into a bowl, and then put in the cooked rabbit meat. Add some mashed garlic, and then some light soy sauce, salt and essence of chicken.

Step 5

Drip in some chili oil and then some sesame oil to mix well to be full of taste with chopsticks.

Step 6

Plate up the stirred well rabbit meat to finish.

Chicken Shreds Mixed with Sesame Paste

Cooking Time	Taste	Culinary Art	Benefits	Suitable for
2 Minutes	Spicy	Mixing	Improve Vitality and Nourish the Blood	Pregnant and Lactating mothers

• Ingredients
chicken breast 200g, ginger 30g, red peppers 15g, shallot 10g

• Seasonings
salt 3g, essence of chicken 1g, sesame paste 10g, sesame oil and cooking wine as needed

How to prepare

Step 1

Add some fresh water to a wok, and put the chicken breast. Add some cooking wine, cover and let it boil. Cook the chicken breast for 10 minutes until cooked before taking it out, and put it in a bowl and let it cool down.

Step 2

Peel and wash the ginger and shred it. Wash the shallots and shred it. Cut the cleaned red pepper into half from the top and remove the seeds, and then cut into shreds.

Step 3

Pat the chicken breast until its flaccid and loose, and then tear it into shreds. Put the chicken shreds in a bowl and add in shredded red pepper, ginger and shallots; add salt, essence of chicken and sesame paste to season well. Stir until all the flavors combine well.

Step 4

Put the well-mixed chicken shreds in a bowl; add a few drops of sesame oil before serving.

CULINARY TIPS

Boil the chicken breast well and ladle out, and put it in ice water to cool it down fast. This makes the flesh more tender.

SEAFOOD & FISH

Shrimps with Cucumber

Cooking Time	Taste	Culinary Art	Benefits	Suitable for
3.5 Minutes	Spicy	Mixing	Lowering Blood Lipid	General

• Ingredients
cucumber 350g, shrimp meat 50g, red pepper 15g, mashed garlic and minced shallot as needed

• Seasonings
salt 4g, essence of chicken 3g, mature vinegar, light soy sauce, chili oil, each for 3ml, sesame oil 2ml, potato starch and cooking oil as needed

How to prepare

Step 1

Cut the cucumber in half and remove seeds and then cut into small pieces for later use; cut the red pepper into half and remove seeds, and cut into small pieces for later use.

Step 2

Cut up the shrimps from the back and remove the "shrimp lines"[5] and put the meat in a bowl; add in some potato starch to mix well, and preserve for 10 minutes.

Step 3

Add wok with an appropriate amount of fresh water to boil up and add in a little cooking oil and salt.

Step 4

Add cucumber and red pepper to boil for 1 minute. Ladle out the boiled cucumber and red pepper, cool down for use later. Add the shrimps, to boil for about 20 seconds, ladle out cooked shrimp meat and cool down for use later.

Step 5

Put the cucumber and red pepper in a bowl and add in shrimp. Add in mashed garlic and minced shallot. Add salt, essence of chicken, mature vinegar and light soy sauce, and then the sesame oil and chili oil to mix well.

Step 6

Plate up to finish.

---

5 shrimp's digestive tract .

Squids with Pepper Shreds

Cooking Time	Taste	Culinary Art	Benefits	Suitable for
4 Minutes	Fresh and Delicious	Mixing	Appetizing and Help Digestion	The Elderly

• Ingredients

squids 200g, green peppers and red peppers each for 15g, mashed garlic 10g

• Seasonings

salt 3g, essence of chicken and potato starch as needed, chili oil, light soy sauce and cooking wine each for 3ml, cooking oil as needed.

How to prepare

Step 1

Wash the red and green peppers and remove the seeds, and cut both into shreds.

Step 2

Cut the treated squids into sections of 4cm long, plate up. Add some salt, essence of chicken and cooking wine to knead well. And then put some potato starch to knead well and pickle for about 5 minute.

Step 3

Add fresh water into a wok and bring to boil with a large flame, add an appropriate amount of cooking oil, and then put in the prepared green and red pepper shreds to mix well and boil up. Ladle out and lay in dish for use later.

Step 4

Put the squid in wok to boil for about 1 minute until cooked, and ladle out to serve up.

Step 5

Get a bowl to put in the squid and then put in the green and red pepper shreds and mashed garlic. Add some salt, essence of chicken, chili oil and light soy sauce.

Step 6

Use chopsticks to mix well and serve up.

Stir-fried Shrimp with Pineapple

Cooking Time	Taste	Culinary Art	Benefits	Suitable for
3 Minutes	Fresh and Delicious	Stir-frying	Heat-clearing and Detoxification	General

• Ingredients
shrimp meat 100g, pineapple 150g, green and red pepper each for 15g, sliced ginger, mashed garlic and chopped scallion as needed

• Seasonings
salt 5g, starchy sauce 10ml, MSG 3g, essence of chicken 3g, cooking wine and cooking oil as needed

How to prepare

Step 1

Wash the pineapple pulp and cut into small chunks; Wash the green and red peppers and cut into pieces.

Step 2

Wash the shrimps and cut into half; add in salt, MSG, starchy sauce to preserve in oil for 5 minutes.

Step 3

Add fresh water into a wok and bring to boil and put in the pineapple pulp for cooking before fishing out.

Step 4

Add shrimps to scramble up until the turning of color to ladle out for later use.

Step 5

Heat some oil in the wok and add sliced ginger, mashed garlic and chopped scallion stalk. Add in the prepared green and red peppers to stir fry quickly to enhance the flavor. Add the boiled shrimps to stir fry evenly. Drip in an appropriate amount of cooking wine.

Step 6

Add the prepared pineapple, and add in salt, essence of chicken to stir fry well for seasoning and dress with starchy sauce. Add some boiled oil.

Step 7

Stir fry evenly to be full of taste and plate up to finish.

Baby Chinese Cabbage with Shrimps and Garlic

Cooking Time	Taste	Culinary Art	Benefits	Suitable for
3 Minutes	Fresh and Delicious	Stir-frying	Refreshing and Brain Fitness	Children

• Ingredients
baby Chinese cabbage 450g, shrimps 150g, carrots 20g, minced garlic as needed

• Seasonings
salt 3g, essence of chicken 2g, whiter sugar 2g, starchy sauce 10ml, cooking wine, sauce of shallot and ginger preserved in wine, garlic oil, cooking oil as needed

How to prepare

Step 1

Cut the cleaned baby Chinese cabbage into sections from the top, and further cut into pieces.

Step 2

Cut up the shrimps from the back and remove the "shrimp lines" and put the meat in a bowl; add in the sauce with shallot and gingered preserved in wine, salt, starchy sauce to mix well, and pickle for about 5 to 6 minutes to be full of taste.

Step 3

Add oil to the wok and Add the shrimps to stir fry quickly and put in the minced garlic to stir fry well.

Step 4

Add the stalk of the prepared baby Chinese cabbage and the sliced carrots to stir fry for about 1 minute. Add the leaves of baby Chinese cabbage to stir fry well. Drip in cooking wine to stir fry, as well as salt, essence of chicken and white sugar to stir fry for 1 minute to be full of taste.

Step 5

Dress with some starchy sauce, and drip in garlic oil before serving.

Step 6

Stir fry to be full of taste and serve up.

CULINARY TIPS

When stir frying the shrimps, use strong flame to stir fry quickly, and do not keep in wok for too long in case of impairing the fresh and tender taste of the shrimps.

The Seething Shrimps

Cooking Time	Taste	Culinary Art	Benefits	Suitable for
3 Minutes	Fresh and Delicious	Stir-frying	Lowering Blood Pressure	The Elderly

• Ingredients
shrimps 300g, dried chili 10g, Sichuan pepper 7g, minced garlic, sliced ginger and chopped scallion as needed

• Seasonings
salt, MSG, essence of chicken, chili oil, thick broad-bean sauce and cooking oil as needed

How to prepare

Step 1
Wash the shrimps and cut the head, whiskers and the feet.

Step 2
Heat some oil in the wok and add minced garlic, sliced ginger and chopped scallion. Add dried chili and Sichuan pepper to stir fry quickly to enhance the flavor. And then add the thick broad-bean sauce to stir fry well.

Step 3
Add an appropriate amount of fresh water, and then some chili oil, as well as salt, MSG and essence of chicken to season well. Add the shrimps to boil for about 1 minute to be cooked and stir fry quickly in wok for a while.

Step 4
Plate up to finish.

> **CULINARY TIPS**
> During stir frying of the seasonings to enhance the flavor, use medium and low flame to fry slowly until there come out the flavor gradually, and then add the shrimps and use a large flame to stir fry quickly, which can make the shrimps full of taste and to ensure the freshness and tenderness of the shrimps.

• Ingredients

shrimp balls 100g, pre-soaked nori 90g, sliced ginger and minced shallot as needed

• Seasonings

salt 3g, essence of chicken 2g, cooking wine, chili powder and cooking oil as needed

How to Prepare

Step 1

Put the wok on the flame and add some cooking oil to heat to 40% to 50% of the oil temperature, and drip in some cooking wine.

Step 2

Add some fresh water and use a large flame to boil. Add salt, essence of chicken and chili powder to season well.

Step 3

Add the shrimp balls to stir well and turn to medium flame to boil until cooked. And then add the nori and sliced ginger, stirring until the broth boils.

Step 4

Ladle out the soup in a bowl and spread on minced shallot to finish.

Cooking Time	Taste	Culinary Art	Benefits	Suitable for
4 Minutes	Fresh and Delicious	Boiling	Boost Immunity	Children

Shrimp Ball Soup with Nori

Fried Cuttlefish with Seasonal Vegetables

Cooking Time	Taste	Culinary Art	Benefits	Suitable for
3 Minutes	Plain	Stir frying	Boost Immunity	General

• Ingredients
Cucurbita pepo(summer squash) 200g, cuttlefish 100g, carrots 80g, onion 50g, red pepper 30g, minced garlic, sliced ginger and chopped scallion stalk as needed

• Seasonings
salt, MSG, cooking wine, oyster sauce, potato starch and starchy sauce as needed

How to prepare

Step 1

Wash the summer squash and cut into slices; do the same to the onions, carrots and red peppers.

Step 2

Shred the prepared cuttlefish; add in cooking wine, salt, MSG and potato starch to pickle for 10 minutes.

Step 3

Boil up fresh water, and add in salt, cooking oil and the prepared carrots to mix well and boil up. Add the cleaned summer squash to mix well and boil for 1 minute to be fully cooked. Ladle out the boiled carrots and the summer squash for later use.

Step 4

Add the prepared cuttlefish; ladle out after boiling for later use.

Step 5

Heat some oil in the wok and add the minced garlic, sliced ginger and chopped scallion stalk to stir fry quickly to enhance the flavor. Add the cuttlefish to stir fry well and add in a little cooking wine, and then the prepared onion and red pepper to stir fry well.

Step 6

Add in the carrots, summer squash, salt, MSG, oyster oil to stir fry well, and add in some starchy sauce to stir fry quickly to be even. Plate up to finish.

CULINARY TIPS

After putting the Cucurbita pepo (summer squash), drip in some vinegar, which can make the sliced summer squash more crispy and tender.

Cuttlefish Rolls with Green Peppers

Cooking Time	Taste	Culinary Art	Benefits	Suitable for
3 Minutes	Spicy	Stir-frying	Boost Immunity	Female

• Ingredients
cuttlefish 100g, green peppers 120g, red peppers 20g, minced garlic and sliced ginger and chopped scallion stalk as needed

• Seasonings
salt, MSG, essence of chicken, cooking wine and starchy sauce as needed

How to prepare

Step 1

Wash green peppers and remove the seeds, cut in shreds; do the same to the red peppers.

Step 2

Shred the prepared cuttlefish; add in cooking wine, salt and MSG to knead even.

Step 3

Add fresh water into the wok and bring to boil and Add the cuttlefish, after boiling to ladle out.

Step 4

Use a large flame and heat up some oil in the wok; add in minced garlic, sliced ginger and chopped scallion stalk to stir fry quickly to enhance the flavor. Add the cuttlefish and add in some cooking wine to stir fry to enhance the flavor. Add in the prepared green and red peppers to stir fry until cooked.

Step 5

Add in salt, MSG, essence of chicken to season well. Dress with some starchy sauce.

Step 6

Stir fry the starched food well, and then plate up to finish.

Fried Squids with Baby cornoung Corn Spears

Cooking Time	Taste	Culinary Art	Benefits	Suitable for
3 Minutes	Fresh and Delicious	Stir-frying	Refreshing and Brain Fitness	General

• Ingredients
squid 300g, young corn spear 150g, sliced ginger, sliced carrots and chopped scallion as needed

• Seasonings
salt, MSG, white sugar, starchy sauce, cooking wine, potato starch and cooking oil as needed

How to prepare

Step 1

Do the crisscross cutting to the treated squid, and further cut into small chunks. Wash the young corn spears and cut in half from the top.

Step 2

Put the squid in a bowl and add in salt, cooking wine and some potato starch; knead well and pickle to enhance flavor

Step 3

Boil the fresh water and put in salt and the young corn spears as well as a little cooking oil, boiling quickly to be cooked and ladle out.

Step 4

Add the squid and boil briefly; ladle out the squid and drain off.

Step 5

Heat some oil in the wok and add sliced ginger, sliced carrots and chopped scallion to stir fry quickly to enhance the flavor. And then add the quick-boiled young corn spears, put in the squid and some cooking wine to stir fry well. Add in salt, MSG and white sugar to stir fry well.

Step 6

Add in a little starchy sauce to stir fry well. Plate up to finish.

CULINARY TIPS

During the cooking of fresh squid, the organs should be removed, since they contain a lot of cholesterol.

Braised Crucian Carp

Cooking Time	Taste	Culinary Art	Benefits	Suitable for
3 Minutes	Fresh and Delicious	Braising	Appetizing and Help Digestion	Pregnant and Lactating Mothers

• Ingredients
one crucian carp, sliced red pepper, shredded ginger and chopped scallion as needed

• Seasonings
salt, MSG, oyster sauce, dark soy sauce, cooking wine, scallion oil, chili oil and potato starch as needed

How to prepare

Step 1

Descale and gut the fish and wash it, do the slant-cutting on the fish, and add in cooking wine, salt and potato starch to spread well.

Step 2

Heat some oil in the wok until it is 60% of the oil temperature, and put in the crucian carp. Deep fry for about 2 minutes until the fish turns a golden color to ladle out.

Step 3

Leave some oil in the wok and put in shredded ginger and chopped scallion stalk to stir fry for flavor. Put in the crucian carp, and drip in cooking wine and Add some fresh water to braise for 1 minute. Add in salt, MSG, oyster sauce and dark soy sauce to season. Add in the prepared red pepper to stir well.

Step 4

Drip in some scallion oil and chili oil to mix well. Braising up the broth into sauce before serving add in some minced shallot to finish.

CULINARY TIPS

When cooking the crucian carp, drip in cooking wine and cover the wok immediately for braising for a while and then add in some water for boiling, which can fully remove the fish odor and enhance the freshness and flavor of the dish.

Braised Crucian Carp with Scallion

Cooking Time	Taste	Culinary Art	Benefits	Suitable for
10 Minutes	Fresh and Delicious	Braising	Improve Vitality and Nourish the Blood	Pregnant and Lactating Mothers

• Ingredients
crucian carp 450g, chopped scallion stalk and sectioned scallion each for 25g, shredded ginger 15g, shredded red pepper 10g

• Seasonings
scallion oil, salt, oyster sauce, dark soy sauce, cooking wine, cooking oil, starch and starchy sauce as needed

Step 1

Descale and gut the fish and wash it clean, and add in cooking wine and salt to knead well. And then spread on starch to knead well; pickle for 10 minutes.

Step 2

Heat some oil in the wok until it is 50%-60% of the oil temperature, and put in the crucian carp. Deep fry for about 1 minute, and keep frying for about 2 minutes until the fish turns golden color on both sides. Ladle out.

Step 3

Leave some oil in the wok and put in shredded ginger and chopped scallion stalk to stir fry for flavor. Add some fresh water, salt, oyster sauce, dark soy sauce and cooking wine to boil.

Step 4

Put in the fried crucian carp, and cover the wok to braise for 3 minutes.

Step 6

Add in the left cooking broth with the prepared shredded red pepper, and add in the starchy sauce to stir well; spread on the prepared sectioned scallion, then add in a little scallion oil to mix well to make it into sticky sauce.

Step 5

Uncover the wok and boil for a while until fully cooked; ladle out the fish and serve up.

Step 7

Serve the prepared sauce on the fish to finish.

CULINARY TIPS

After the treatment of the crucian carp, drip in a little yellow rice wine for pickling for a while, This can remove the fish odor and enhance the freshness and flavor of the dish, and make the meat of fish much more delicious.

Turnip and Crucian Soup

Cooking Time	Taste	Culinary Art	Benefits	Suitable for
18 Mintues	Fresh and Delicious	Boiling	Appetizing and Help Digestion	Pregnant and Lactating mothers

• Ingredients
one crucian, turnip 250g, ginger shreds and minced shallot as needed

• Seasonings
salt 5g, essence of chicken 3g, cooking wine, cooking oil and chili powder as needed

How to prepare

Step 1

Slice and shred the peeled and washed turnips.

Step 2

Heat some oil in the wok and add the ginger shreds to stir fry to enhance the flavor. Put in the descaled, gutted and cleaned crucian to fry briefly while turning the wok.

Step 3

Drip in the cooking wine and add in enough hot water. Add some salt and essence of chicken. Cover and boil for 15 minutes over a large flame.

Step 4

Uncover the wok and put in the turnip shreds and boil for about 2 minutes. Add in an appropriate amount of chili powder.

Step 5

Transfer the mixture into an earthenware pot and put it on a large flame, and boil.

Step 6

Turn off the flaming, and spread on the prepared minced shallot. Move the earthenware pot away from the flame.

CULINARY TIPS

When cooking the crucian, you should control the flame and the oil temperature well, during which you should use a large flame at first and later turn to medium flame, and always keep the broth boiling until the broth turns into a milky color.

Braised Mackerel

Cooking Time	Taste	Culinary Art	Benefits	Suitable for
2 Minutes	Fresh and Delicious	Stir-frying	Boost Immunity	General

• Ingredients
mackerel 180g, shredded ginger, shredded black mushroom, mashed garlic and chopped scallion as needed

• Seasonings
salt, MSG, white sugar, oyster sauce, light soy sauce, dark soy sauce, soup-stock, potato starch, starchy sauce, cooking wine and cooking oil as needed

How to prepare

Step 1

Add on the treated mackerel with salt, MSG, cooking wine and light soy sauce for pickling for about 7 to 8 minutes. Spread on the mackerel with potato starch to knead well.

Step 2

Put the mackerel in a heated wok with hot oil and turn to medium flame; after frying for about 1 minute, flip over the fish and fry on the other side for another minute until fully cooked to ladle out.

Step 3

Leave some oil in the wok and put in shredded ginger, shredded black mushrooms and mashed garlic to stir fry for flavor. Add some soup-stock and add in salt, MSG, light soy sauce and white sugar, and then drip in oyster oil and dark soy sauce to stir well and boil up.

Step 4

Put in the mackerel and braise for about 2 minutes to be full of taste. Ladle out the cooked fish for later use. Leave the broth in wok.

Step 5

Add starchy sauce to the broth to mix well and add some hot oil; spread on some chopped scallion to make the sticky sauce.

Step 6

Serve the sauce on the fish to finish.

CULINARY TIPS

During the deep frying of the mackerel, the heat should be controlled well, which is to deep fry with medium and low flame. After it is fried well, use a large flame for more quick-frying before ladling out, so as to make the fried fish crispy outside while a tender meat inside.

Steamed Bass

Cooking Time	Taste	Culinary Art	Benefits	Suitable for
9 Minutes	Plain	Steaming	Improve Vitality and Nourish the Blood	Pregnant and Lactating Mothers

• Ingredients
bass 400g, shallot 10g, red pepper 15g, chopped scallion stalk, shredded ginger and sliced ginger as needed

• Seasonings
soy sauce 30ml, cooking oil and chili powder as needed

How to prepare

Step 1

Descale and gut the bass and wash it; cut open the bass from the spine; wash the shallot and cut into shreds; Wash the red pepper and cut into shreds.

Step 2

Lay the prepared bass on a dish, put on the sliced ginger and chopped scallion stalk. Put the dish in a steamer and cover; steam on a large flame for 7 minutes until fully cooked.

Step 3

Uncover the steamer and get the bass out; pick off the sliced ginger and chopped scallion stalk, and then spread on shredded ginger, shredded shallot and shredded red pepper. Spread on an appropriate amount of chili powder.

Step 4

Add in some cooking oil into the wok and heat up to 70% of the oil temperature. Serve the hot oil on the fish.

Step 5

Add in soy sauce in wok and heat. Serve it on the margin of the dish to finish.

Fish Fillets in Hot Sauce

Cooking Time	Taste	Culinary Art	Benefits	Suitable for
10 Minutes	Spicy	Boiling	Anti-hypertension and Anti-diabetics	People with Hypertension

• Ingredients

grass carp meat 550g, Chinese prickly ash 1g, dry red pepper 1g, ginger slices 10g, garlic slices 8g, chopped scallion stalk 10g, soybean sprouts 30g, and minced shallot as needed

• Seasonings

salt 6g, essence of chicken 6g, starchy sauce 10ml, chili oil 15ml, thick broad-bean sauce 30g, cooking wine 3ml, Sichuan pepper (zanthoxylum) oil chili powder, seed powder of Chinese prickly ash and cooking oil as needed

How to prepare

Step 1

Cut off the head of grass carp and chop into chunks, and then remove the spine of the fish and chop into chunks. Remove the belly bones, and chop into chunks. Cut the fish into slices in a slant way.

Step 2

Add some salt, essence of chicken and chili powder to the fish bones to pickle for 10 minutes. Add some salt, starchy sauce, essence of chicken, chili powder and oil to the fish to pickle for 10 minutes.

Step 3

Heat some oil in the wok and add ginger, garlic and shallot to stir fry to enhance the flavor. Add in dry red pepper, Chinese prickly ash, and the fish bones to stir fry briefly, and add in cooking wine.

Step 4

Add in about 800ml of fresh water. Drip in chili oil, Sichuan pepper (zanthoxylum) oil and thick broad-bean sauce to stir well. Cover and boil with medium flame for about 4 minutes.

Step 5

Uncover the wok and put in soybean sprouts. Add in salt and essence of chicken to stir well.

Step 6

Ladle out the materials into a bowl and leave the broth in wok. Add the fillets, and stir well; boil on a large flame for 1 minute.

Step 7

Ladle out the fillets and the broth into a bowl; spread on minced shallot and seed powder of Chinese prickly ash.

Step 8

Add in some cooking oil to the wok and boil to 60% of the oil temperature. Serve the hot oil on the fillets to finish.

Fish Head Soup with Gastrodia Elata

Cooking Time	Taste	Culinary Art	Benefits	Suitable for
11 Minutes	Fresh and Delicious	Stewing	Refreshing and Brain Fitness	General

• Ingredients
fish head (bighead carp or grass carp) 250g, sliced ginger 20g, gastrodia elata 5g, medlar 2g

• Seasonings
salt, cooking oil, essence of chicken as needed

How to prepare

Step 1

Put the wok on a large flame and add in oil to heat; add sliced ginger to stir fry quickly to enhance the flavor.

Step 2

Put in the cleaned fish head and fry until they turn golden-brown to lay on a dish for later use.

Step 3

Get a cleaned earthenware pot to add boiled water and put in gastrodia elata, and then put in sliced ginger and the fish head. Add in some salt and boil on a large flame. Add in some essence of chicken.

Step 4

Cover the pot and turn to medium flame to stew for 8 minutes.

Step 5

Uncover the pot and put in medlar; go on stewing with medium flame for a while.

Step 6

Turn off the flame and get the earthenware pot off the cooking bench.

CULINARY TIPS

Do not add too much oil when frying the fish. In that case the fried fish head is too greasy and affect the taste.

Sweet and Sour Yellow Croaker

Cooking Time	Taste	Culinary Art	Benefits	Suitable for
7 Minutes	Fresh and Delicious	Deep-frying	Appetizing and Help Digestion	General

• Ingredients
yellow croaker 200g, tomato juice 30g, minced red pepper, mashed garlic and minced shallot as needed

• Seasonings
salt, whiter sugar, starchy sauce and starch as needed

Step 1

Descale and gut the fish and wash it, do the crisscross cutting to the fish, and add in some salt to knead well, and spread on some starch and also knead well.

Step 2

Add oil into the wok and heat up to 60% of the oil temperature; put in the prepared yellow croaker to deep-fry with medium flame for 2 to 3 minutes until the fish turns to a golden color and is fully cooked. Ladle out the yellow croaker onto a dish for later use.

Step 3

Leave some oil in the wok and put in mashed garlic and minced red pepper to stir fry. This will enhance the flavor. Add the tomato juice and mix well; add in white sugar and mix well. then add in some fresh water to boil up.

Step 4

Dress with some starchy sauce and mix well into thick sauce and serve on the fish to finish.

CULINARY TIPS

Before cooking, you can put the yellow croaker in milk for a while, which not only dispels the fish odor, but also can enhance the freshness and flavor of the fish. In addition, during the dressing with starchy sauce, you can add in some white vinegar, which can also enhance the fragrance.

Winter Bamboo Shoots Soup with Seafood

Cooking Time	Taste	Culinary Art	Benefits	Suitable for
45 Minutes	Fresh and Delicious	Boiling	Appetizing and Help Digestion	The Elderly

• Ingredients

winter bamboo shoots 120g, squid 180g, some sliced ginger, shrimps, and "Shanghai Qing" (the pakchoi cabbage) [6] as needed

• Seasonings

salt 3g, essence of chicken, cooking wine, chili powder and sesame oil as needed

How to prepare

Step 1

Peel the squid and do the crisscross cutting on it, and then cut into slices. Cut the washed winter bamboo shoots into slices.

Step 2

Add some fresh water in wok and put in ginger shreds. Put in sliced winter bamboo shoots and dried peeled shrimps to stir well and boil. Add the squid slices and add in salt and essence of chicken. Stir well and boil for a short period.

Step 3

Add in some cooking wine to stir well, and put in the washed "Shanghai Qing" pakchoi cabbage to stir well. Add in some chili powder to mix well.

Step 4

Drip in some sesame oil and stir well, ladle out in a bowl to finish.

6 a kind of pakchoi cabbage, brassica chinensis.

CULINARY TIPS

Winter bamboo shoot contains protein, amino acids, vitamins, sugars, and calcium, iron, phosphorus and other minerals, which is good for clearing heat and eliminating phlegm, adjusting the vitality and harmonizing stomach, treating diabetes and inducing dieresis, helping digestion and prevention of constipation, etc. In addition, winter bamboo shoot is the food that contains low fat and low calories, and is the appropriate food for losing weight and slimming.

BEANS

Mapo Tofu (spicy bean curd)

Cooking Time	Taste	Culinary Art	Benefits	Suitable for
4 Minutes	Spicy	Stir-frying	Appetizing and Help Digestion	General

• Ingredients
tender bean curd 500g, minced stewed beef 70g, mashed garlic and minced shallot as needed

• Seasonings
cooking oil 35ml, thick broad-bean sauce 35g, salt, essence of chicken, MSG, chili oil, zanthoxylum oil, oyster sauce, dark soy sauce and starchy sauce as needed

How to prepare

Step 1

Cut the bean curd into small cubes.

Step 2

Add 1500ml of fresh water into the wok and bring to boil and then add in salt. Add the bean curd to boil for about 1 minute to be full of taste, and ladle out for later use.

Step 3

Put the wok on strong flame and add in oil to heat. Add in mashed garlic to stir fry to enhance flavor. Add the minced stewed beef to stir fry for about 1 minute until the turning of color.

Step 4

Add in thick broad-bean sauce to stir fry to enhance the flavor. Add in 200ml of fresh water, as well as the oyster sauce, dark soy sauce to stir fry well. Add in salt, essence of chicken and MSG to stir fry to be tasty.

Step 5

Add the bean curd, add in chili oil and Sichuan pepper (zanthoxylum) oil to stir fry gently, and then use a low flame to boil for about 2 minutes to enhance flavor. Add in some starchy sauce, and spread on minced shallot to stir fry.

Step 6

Plate up and spread on some minced shallot again to dress up.

CULINARY TIPS

Put the tender bean curd in hot water for quick boiling, so that the bean curd can stand the cooking and will not get mashed easily.

Bean Curd in Brown Sauce

Cooking Time	Taste	Culinary Art	Benefits	Suitable for
4 Minutes	Fresh and Delicious	Stir-frying	Appetizing and Help Digestion	General

• Ingredients
firm bean curd 300g, lean pork 40g, pre-soaked black mushrooms 30g, sliced ginger, sliced garlic and chopped scallion as needed

• Seasonings
salt 3g, MSG 3g, white sugar 3g, essence of chicken 3g, dark soy sauce 3ml, cooking wine, starchy sauce, thick broad-bean sauce and cooking oil as needed

How to prepare

Step 1

Cut the bean curd into small cubes; wash the black mushrooms and cut into shreds.

Step 2

Heat some oil in the wok until it is 50% of the oil temperature, and add the bean curd to deep-fry for about 2 minutes until the surface of bean curd turn a golden color to ladle out.

Step 3

Leave some oil in wok to add in sliced ginger, sliced garlic and chopped scallion and black mushrooms, and then add the shredded pork to stir fry for flavor; add some cooking wine to stir fry well.

Step 4

Add in some fresh water, and the oyster sauce, salt, MSG, white sugar, essence of chicken, thick broad-bean sauce and dark soy sauce to stir fry well.

Step 5

Add the bean curd to boil for about 2 minutes to be tasty and add in the starchy sauce.

Step 6

Add in some boiled oil to stir fry well; plate up to finish.

CULINARY TIPS

Add the soup-stock in to the wok which is better to flood over the food, or if too less, the would stick to the wok.

Bean curd Balls

Cooking Time	Taste	Culinary Art	Benefits	Suitable for
3 Minutes	Plain	Deep frying	Heat-clearing and Detoxification	General

• Ingredients
bean curd 200g, celery 50g, one egg, leaves of rape as needed

• Seasonings
essence of chicken, salt, potato starch, cooking oil, chili powder and sesame oil as needed

How to prepare

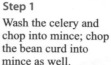

Step 1

Wash the celery and chop into mince; chop the bean curd into mince as well.

Step 2

Put the minced bean curd into a bowl and add in egg to stir well; Put in essence of chicken and salt to mix well. Add the minced celery to mix well. Spread on the potato starch to stir well, and then add in chili powder and sesame oil to stir well.

Step 3

Add in fresh water and drip in cooking oil to boil; put in the cleaned leaves of rape to boil quickly and ladle out.

Step 4

Knead the minced celery and bean curd into balls.

Step 5

Add oil to the wok and bring to heat to about 50% of the oil temperature, and then put the balls into the wok for deep-frying for about 2 minutes to be cooked; ladle out for use later.

Step 6

Arrange the leaves of rape around the edge of the dish, and lay on the dish with the fried bean curd balls.

CULINARY TIPS

When putting the bean curd balls in wok for deep-frying, you should control the oil heat to be around 50%, and use medium and low flame for deep-frying, soaking the balls fully, so that the balls will taste even better.

Steamed Bean curd with Shrimps

Cooking Time	Taste	Culinary Art	Benefits	Suitable for
8 Minutes	Fresh and Delicious	Steaming	Boost Immunity	General

• Ingredients
bean curd 350g, shrimp meat 150g, minced shallot as needed

• Seasonings
salt, MSG, essence of chicken, potato starch and sesame oil as needed

How to prepare

Step 1
Wash the bean curd and cut into small cubes, arrange on a dish; spread on some salt for use later.

Step 2
Wash the shrimps and cut into dices; add in salt, MSG and essence of chicken. And then add in some potato starch to stir well. Drip in sesame oil and cooking oil to mix well, and let it marinate for 10 minutes.

Step 3
Put the preserved shrimps on the bean curd and then put in the steamer; cover and steam on a strong flame for about 6 minutes.

Step 4
Take out the steamed bean curd with shrimps from the steamer and drain off the steamed juice; spread on minced shallot.

Step 5
Heat up some oil in the wok and then serve on the shrimps; plate up to finish.

VEGETABLES

Bean Sprouts with Red Peppers

Cooking Time	Taste	Culinary Art	Benefits	Suitable for
3 Minutes	Spicy	Mixing	Beauty and Rejuvenation	Female

• Ingredients

soybean sprouts 150g, red pepper 15g, chopped scallion 10g

• Seasonings

salt 3g, MSG 1g, white sugar 1g, mature vinegar 10ml, sesame oil and cooking oil as needed

How to prepare

Step 1

Wash the red peppers and remove the seeds; and then cut into shreds.

Step 2

Add about 1000ml of fresh water in the wok to boil up and then add in some cooking oil; add the cleaned soybean sprouts to scramble up and boil for about 2 minutes.

Step 3

Add in the prepared red peppers and then the chopped scallion to stir well.

Step 4

After boiling for a while, put the mixture in a bowl and then put in salt, MSG and white sugar. Add in some vinegar and drip in a little sesame oil.

Step 5

Stir well the materials with chopsticks; plate up the stirred well materials to finish.

- **Ingredients**

purple cabbage 600g, shredded carrots 30g, green pepper rings 30g, mashed garlic 30g

- **Seasonings**

salt 3g, essence of chicken, sesame oil and cooking oil as needed

How to Prepare

Step 1

Wash the purple cabbage and cut into shreds.

Step 2

Add 1500ml of fresh water into the wok and bring to boil and then add in some cooking oil.

Step 3

Add the purple cabbage and shredded carrots to boil briefly for about 1 minute to be cooked and ladle out.

Step 4

Put the boiled purple cabbage and shredded carrots in a bowl and add in mashed garlic, green pepper rings. Add in salt, essence of chicken and stir with chopsticks to mix efficiently.

Step 5

Drip in some sesame oil to mix well and serve up.

Cooking Time	Taste	Culinary Art	Benefits	Suitable for
2 Minutes	Mixing/ cold salad	Stirring	Appetizing and Help Digestion	General

Purple Cabbage Mixed with Assorted Vegetables

Bitter Melon Mixed with Mashed Garlic

Cooking Time	Taste	Culinary Art	Benefits	Suitable for
4 Minutes	Plain	Mixing	Heat-clearing and Detoxification	Pregnant and Lactating Mothers

• Ingredients
bitter melon 300g, mashed garlic 10g

• Seasonings
salt 3g, MSG 1g, white vinegar 1g, baking soda and sesame oil as needed

How to prepare

Step 1

Wash the bitter melon and cut in half; remove the pulp and seeds, and then cut into strips.

Step 2

Add in some fresh water to boil up and then put in baking soda, salt and the bitter melon to mix well; boil for about 2 minutes.

Step 3

Ladle out the boiled bitter melon and put in cool water for a while.

Step 4

Ladle out the bitter melon and put in a bowl; add in mashed garlic, as well as salt, MSG and white sugar. And then drip in some sesame oil, use chopsticks to stir well.

Step 5

Put the stirred bitter melon on a dish to finish.

• Ingredients
cucumber 350g, red pepper 20g, chrysanthemum, mashed garlic and minced shallot as needed

• Seasonings
salt 3g, mature vinegar 8ml, essence of chicken 2g, light soy sauce and sesame oil as needed

How to Prepare

Step 1

Wash the red peppers and cut into rings

Step 2

Wash and smash the cucumber, and then cut into sections.

Step 3

Put the cucumber in a bowl and add in red pepper rings and the cleaned chrysanthemum. Add in mashed garlic, as well as salt, essence of chicken; and then add in mature vinegar. Put in the minced shallot and light soy sauce to mix well.

Step 4

Add in some sesame oil and mix well. Plate up the cucumber to finish.

Cooking Time	Taste	Culinary Art	Benefits	Suitable for
2 Minutes	Plain	Mixing	Anti-hypertension and Anti-diabetics	The Diabetic

Smashed Cucumber Mixed with Garlic Sauce

Turnip Shreds in Premium Recipe

Cooking Time	Taste	Culinary Art	Benefits	Suitable for
2 Minutes	Plain	Mixing	Appetizing and Help Digestion	General

• Ingredients
turnip 300g, dried peeled shrimps 10g, red peppers 15g

• Seasonings
salt 3g, essence of chicken 2g, sesame oil 2ml

How to prepare

Step 1

Wash the turnip and cut into slices and further into shreds. Wash the red pepper remove seeds and then cut into shreds.

Step 2

Add 1000ml of fresh water into the wok and bring to boil and put in dried peeled shrimps. After boiling for a while, ladle out. Add the prepared turnip shreds, scramble up and boil for 2 minutes until cooked.

Step 3

Ladle out the boiled turnip shreds and put in a bowl; add in red pepper shreds; add the boiled shrimps, add in salt, essence of chicken as well as some sesame oil to mix and stir well.

Step 4

Plate up the well-mixed food to finish.

• Ingredients
snow peas 200g, red pepper 20g

• Seasonings
salt 3g, essence of chicken 2g, cooking oil and
sesame oil as needed

How to Prepare

Step 1
Cut the red pepper in
half from the top to
remove the seeds and
further cut into shreds.

Step 2
Add fresh water into the
wok and bring to boil
and add in some cooking
oil; add the cleaned
snow peas to boil for
about 2 minutes until
cooked to ladle out and
drain off.

Step 3
Put the boiled snow
peas in a bowl and
add in salt, essence of
chicken and sesame oil;
and then add red pepper
shreds; use chopsticks
to stir well.

Step 4
Plate up the food to
finish.

Cooking Time	Taste	Culinary Art	Benefits	Suitable for
2 Minutes	Spicy	Mixing	Beauty and Slimming	Female

Snow Peas Mixed with Red Peppers

Asparagus Mixed with Color Peppers

Cooking Time	Taste	Culinary Art	Benefits	Suitable for
3 Minutes	Plain	Mixing	Heat-clearing and Detoxification	General

• Ingredients
asparagus 250g, color peppers 20g, mashed garlic and minced shallot as needed

• Seasonings
salt 3g, essence of chicken 2g, light soy sauce 5ml, sesame oil 3ml and cooking oil as needed

How to prepare

Step 1

Wash the color peppers and cut in half from the top, and then cut into strips and then the dices. Wash and peel the asparagus, and then cut into sections of 3cm long. Put the cut materials in dishes separately for use later.

Step 2

Add in wok with fresh water to boil up on a large flame. Add in some cooking oil and salt. Add the asparagus to cook for about 2 minutes until cooked, and then put in the prepared color peppers to boil for about half a minute to be just cooked.

Step 3

Ladle out the boiled asparagus and color pepper to put in a bowl; add in mashed garlic and minced shallot; and then add in an appropriate amount of salt, light soy sauce and essence of chicken.

Step 4

Drip in some sesame oil and stir well with spoon. Plate up to finish.

CULINARY TIPS

The folic acid in asparagus is vulnerable in the environment of high temperature, therefore, the asparagus should not be cooked for too long, you may lose the folic acid in asparagus.

- **Ingredients**
eggplant 200g, flour 150g

- **Seasonings**
salt, MSG, cooking oil as needed

How to Prepare

Step 1

Peel, wash and slice the eggplant. Put the eggplant slices in water and add in salt to mix well; pickle for 5 minutes to be full of taste.

Step 2

Mix the flour with some salt, MSG and some fresh water to blend well into paste. Dip the eggplant slices with the flour paste.

Step 3

Put the wok with enough oil on a strong flame and bring to heat; and put in the eggplant slices for frying with low flame. Add in some cooking oil during the frying, and flip over the slices when one side turns golden.

Step 4

Fry the other side of the slices into golden as well. Add in some cooking oil again, and use a low flame to fry further until the slices turn fully cooked.

Step 5

Plate up to finish.

CULINARY TIPS

The flour paste should not be too watery, or the eggplant slices cannot be pasted well, and they will further become oily after deep-drying, and taste too greasy. In addition, the flour paste can be added in with some yolk liquid, so that the eggplant slices will turn golden after the deep frying and taste crispy and tender.

Cooking Time	Taste	Culinary Art	Benefits	Suitable for
7 Minutes	Salty	Frying	Appetizing and Help Digestion	General

Fried Sliced Eggplant

Kung Pao Eggplant (spicy diced eggplant with peanuts)

Cooking Time	Taste	Culinary Art	Benefits	Suitable for
2 Minutes	Spicy	Stir-frying	Provides Protection Against Cancer	People with gastro-intestinal trouble

• Ingredients
eggplant 150g, peanuts 50g, dried chili 10g, chopped scallion, sliced ginger and mashed garlic as needed

• Seasonings
salt 2g, MSG, thick broad-bean sauce, cooking wine, potato starch, starchy sauce and cooking oil as needed

How to prepare

Step 1

Wash and peel the eggplant, and cut into dices. Wash the scallion and cut into dices as well.

Step 2

Add the cleaned peanuts in boiling water; add in some salt to boil up. Ladle out the boiled peanuts.

Step 3

Add some oil into the wok and bring to heat to about 40% of the oil temperature; add the peanuts. Deep-fry with low flame for about 2 minutes to be cooked and then ladle out.

Step 4

Spread potato starch on the diced eggplant and then mix well.

Step 5

 Add the egg plant to the hot wok to deep-fry with low flame for 1 minute until turning golden; ladle out the fried eggplant dices.

Step 6

Leave some oil in wok and put in sliced ginger, mashed garlic, chopped scallion and chili pepper to stir fry quickly to enhance the flavor. Add in the eggplant dices and then the salt, MSG, thick broad-bean sauce and cooking wine. After stir frying well, add in a little fresh water to mix and to enhance the flavor.

Step 7

Add in starchy sauce to mix well and Add the peanuts to stir fry well. Plate up to finish.

Chili and Sour Shredded Potato

Cooking Time	Taste	Culinary Art	Benefits	Suitable for
3 Minutes	Spicy	Stir-frying	Slimming and Expelling of Toxin	Female

• Ingredients
potato 200g, red pepper and shallot as needed, salt 3g, white sugar, essence of chicken, white vinegar, sesame oil and cooking oil as needed

• Seasonings
salt 3g, white sugar, essence of chicken, white vinegar, sesame oil and cooking oil as needed

How to prepare

Step 1

Cut the potato in shreds and put in a bowl with fresh water to preserve. Cut the red pepper into shreds as well and the shallot into sections.

Step 2

Add oil into the wok and brig to heat and add the shredded potato and chopped scallion stalk to stir fry well. Add in some salt, white sugar and essence of chicken to mix well and stir fry for about 1 minute, and then add some white vinegar to stir fry.

Step 3

Add the shredded red pepper and chopped shallot to stir fry. Drip in some sesame oil.

Step 4

Plate up to finish.

• Ingredients

fresh niblets (corn) 100g, color pepper 50g, green pepper 20g, sliced ginger, mashed garlic and chopped scallion stalk as needed

• Seasonings

salt 3g, starchy sauce 10ml, MSG 3g, essence of chicken and cooking oil as needed

How to Prepare

Step 1

Wash the color pepper clean and cut half from the top to remove the seeds, and then cut into strips and further into dices. Do the same to the cleaned green pepper. Put the color pepper and green pepper dices into a dish.

Step 2

Add water into the wok and bring to boil and add in salt and cooking oil to stir well. Add the fresh niblets to boil briefly. Add the diced color pepper and green pepper. After boiling up, ladle out for use later.

Step 3

Heat up some oil in the wok and Add sliced ginger, mashed garlic and chopped scallion stalk to stir fry quickly to enhance the flavor. Add the boiled color pepper, green pepper and nib lets to stir fry well. Add in salt, essence of chicken and MSG to stir fry well.

Step 4

Add in starchy sauce and stir fry to be full of taste. Plate up to finish.

Cooking Time	Taste	Culinary Art	Benefits	Suitable for
3 Minutes	Plain	Stir-frying	Lowering Blood Lipid	General

Stir-fried Corn with Color Peppers

Stir-fried Chinese Flowering Cabbage with Garlic

Cooking Time	Taste	Culinary Art	Benefits	Suitable for
2 Minutes	Plain	Stir frying	Heat-clearing and Detoxification	Children

• Ingredients
Chinese flowering cabbage 400g, mashed garlic 15g

• Seasonings
salt 5g, starchy sauce 10ml, MSG 3g, white sugar 3g, cooking wine and cooking oil as needed

How to prepare

Step 1

Wash the Chinese flowering cabbage clean and trim neat.

Step 2

Add in some fresh water in wok and use a large flame to boil up; add in some cooking oil, salt, and then put in the Chinese flowering cabbage to stir well. Boil quickly to be just cooked and then ladle out.

Step 3

Clean up the wok and put in an appropriate amount of cooking oil; after heating, add mashed garlic to stir fry quickly to enhance the flavor. Add the Chinese flowering cabbage to stir fry well. Add in salt, MSG, white sugar and cooking wine to stir well. And then add in some starchy sauce to stir fry and to enhance the flavor.

Step 4

Plate up the well fried Chinese flowering cabbage and serve on the original sauce from the wok to finish.

CULINARY TIPS

Once poured into the hot wok, the Chinese flowering cabbage should not be stir-fried for too long, in case that there is too much moisture coming out which will affect the look and taste.

Braised Bamboo Shoots

Cooking Time	Taste	Culinary Art	Benefits	Suitable for
5 Minutes	Plain	Braising	Appetizing and Helps Digestion	General

• Ingredients
bamboo shoots 350g, chopped garlic sprouts 120g, sliced red pepper as needed

• Seasonings
salt 3g, MSG, white sugar, oyster oil and starchy sauce as needed

How to prepare

Step 1
Peel and wash the bamboo shoots and then cut into pieces.

Step 2
Add fresh water into a wok and bring to boil, and then add in salt and MSG; add the bamboo shoots; after boiling up of the water, ladle out.

Step 3
Leave some oil in the wok, and then add the chopped garlic sprouts and the sliced red pepper to stir fry briefly. Add the prepared bamboo shoots to stir fry well. Add in salt, MSG, white sugar and oyster oil to stir fry well and cover the wok to braise for a while.

Step 4
Add in some starchy sauce and then drip in hot oil to stir fry well. Plate up to finish.

• Ingredients

pumpkin 200g, red dates as needed

How to Prepare

Step 1

Peel and wash the pumpkin and cut into small pieces. Wash the red dates clean and cut up to remove the core.

Step 2

Put the pumpkin in a dish and put on the prepared red dates. Put in a steamer.

Step 3

Cover the steamer and steam with medium flame for about 15 minutes until fully cooked.

Step 4

Uncover the steamer and get out the food.. Plate up to finish.

CULINARY TIPS

During the steaming of pumpkins with red dates, people can determine the steaming time according to their own taste; if someone likes to eat the steamed pumpkin with extremely soft pulp, he or she can prolong the steaming time appropriately, with low flame.

Cooking Time	Taste	Culinary Art	Benefits	Suitable for
18 Minutes	Sweet	Steaming	Anti-hypertension and Anti-diabetics	Female

Steamed Pumpkin with Red Dates

Boiled White Mushroom and Broccoli with Black Pepper

Cooking Time	Taste	Culinary Art	Benefits	Suitable for
4 Minutes	Fresh and Delicious	Boiling	Boost Immunity	Female

• Ingredients
the white mushroom[8] 50g, broccoli 60g, black pepper 5g, red pepper shreds as needed

• Seasonings
salt, essence of chicken, white sugar, sesame oil, cooking oil, starchy sauce as needed

How to prepare

Step 1

Slice the washed white mushrooms, and cut the washed broccoli into pieces of bulb lets.

Step 2

Add in fresh water in wok and put in salt and a little cooking oil. Boil on a large flame. Add the white mushroom in wok. Put in the broccoli to stir well. Boil the white mushroom and broccoli till cooked and ladle out.

Step 3

Heat up some oil in the wok and put in the black pepper to stir fry for flavor. Add in some fresh water to boil up and put in salt. Add in essence of chicken, white sugar to mix well. Add the boiled broccoli and white mushroom, and stir fry evenly.

Step 4

Spread in the red pepper shreds, and add in some starchy sauce to mix well. Drip in some sesame oil to stir well. Plate up to finish.

---

8 White mushroom here is the tricholomagambosum.

> **CULINARY TIPS**
> During the boiling of broccoli, it should not take too long, or the taste will be affected.

• Ingredients

pre-soaked red beans 30g, fresh niblets (corn) 40g, common yam rhizome 60g, celery 30g, green bell pepper 20g, sliced ginger and mashed garlic as needed

• Seasonings

salt, MSG, white sugar, starchy sauce and cooking oil as needed

How to Prepare

Step 1

Peel the rhizome, wash and cut into dices. Wash the celery and green bell peppers and cut into dices.

Step 2

Boil the fresh water in wok and add in cooking oil, salt, fresh niblets, the rhizome, celery and the chopped green bell pepper to boil briefly. And then put in red beans to stir well. Ladle out after boiling..

Step 3

Clean the wok and add oil and heat ; put in sliced ginger, mashed garlic to stir fry for flavor, and then put in the prepared rhizome dices, celery dices, green bell pepper dices, red beans and niblets. Add in some salt, MSG and white sugar to stir fry well.

Step 4

Add in a little starchy sauce to stir fry well, and plate up to finish.

CULINARY TIPS

After peeled, the surface of the common yam rhizome would be oxidized and will turn brown. To prevent this, the common yam rhizome can be put into salt water immediately once peeled.

Cooking Time	Taste	Culinary Art	Benefits	Suitable for
8 Minutes	Plain	Stir-frying	Slimming and Expelling of Toxin	Female

Jin Yu Man Tang (Prosperity of "Gold" and "Jade")

Deep-fried Lotus Root Sandwiches

Cooking Time	Taste	Culinary Art	Benefits	Suitable for
4 Minutes	Plain	Deep-frying	Boost Immunity	General

• Ingredients
lotus root 250g, minced pork 100g, one egg

• Seasonings
cooking oil 30ml, salt 3g, potato starch 2g, essence of chicken, white vinegar and cooking wine as needed

How to prepare

Step 1

Crack the egg into a bowl and add in potato starch to beat up.

Step 2

Peel and wash the lotus root and cut into slices.

Step 3

Add on the minced pork with salt and essence of chicken to stir well. Add in potato starch and cooking wine to mix well; preserve for 10 minutes.

Step 4

Add fresh water into the wok and bring to boil, and then add the lotus root slices; add in white vinegar and salt to mix well and boil for about 2 minutes until cooked to ladle out.

Step 5

Pave a dish with a layer of potato starch and put on the lotus root slices, and then spread on the potato starch again. Serve on each piece of the lotus root slice with some minced pork and then clamp with another piece of the lotus root. This is to make the "lotus root sandwiches".

Step 6

Spread on the "lotus root sandwiches" with some potato starch as well and dress with the mixed egg liquid.

Step 7

Put the "lotus root sandwiches" into wok with boiling oil for deep-frying with low flame for about 2 minutes to be fully cooked; ladle out the fried "lotus root sandwiches".

Step 8

Arrange well on a dish to finish.

CULINARY TIPS

Lotus root contains less sugar, while it is abundant in vitamin C and dietary fiber, which are beneficial to people with hepatopathy, constipation and diabetes.

Simmered Potatoes

Cooking Time	Taste	Culinary Art	Benefits	Suitable for
15 Minutes	Fresh and Delicious	Simmering	Appetizing and Helps Digestion	Pregnant and Lactating Mothers

• Ingredients
potatoes 300g, green pepper and red pepper each for 20g, mashed garlic and chopped scallion stalk as needed

• Seasonings
salt 3g, starchy sauce 10ml, essence of chicken 3g, white sugar 3g, dark soy sauce 3ml, thick broad-bean sauce, oyster sauce and cooking oil as needed

How to prepare

Step 1

Wash the green pepper and red pepper and cut into strips from the top. Peel and wash the potatoes and cut into small chunks.

Step 3

Heat up some oil in the wok and put in mashed garlic and chopped scallion stalk to stir fry quickly to enhance the flavor. Add the potatoes and stir fry well.

Step 5

Uncover the wok and add the prepared green and red pepper; stir fry well.

Step 7

Uncover the wok and add in some starchy sauce. Go on stir-frying in the wok to reduce the broth into sauce.

Step 2

Add in fresh water in wok and bring to boil, add in salt, and put in potatoes to stir well; boil on a large flame for about 3 minutes to be just cooked. Ladle out the boiled potatoes.

Step 4

Add in about 200ml of fresh water, and then the oyster sauce, dark soy sauce, salt, essence of chicken and white sugar. Add in thick broad-bean sauce to stir fry evenly and to season well. Cover the wok and simmer with low flame for about 10 minutes until cooked.

Step 6

Cover and simmer on a low flame for 3 more minutes until the potatoes are fully cooked and flaccid so it can be easily smashed.

Step 8

Plate up to finish.

CULINARY TIPS

Potato is a common food on the dining table, which can either be served as main food, or a vegetable. It contains abundant vitamin B and plenty of dietary fibers of quality, as well as the nutrition of trace elements, protein, fat and high quality of starch, etc.

Lantern Eggplant

Cooking Time	Taste	Culinary Art	Benefits	Suitable for
12 Minutes	Sour	Steaming	Heat-clearing and Detoxification	General

• Ingredients
eggplant 500g, mashed garlic and minced shallot as needed

• Seasonings
salt 3g, mature vinegar, white sugar, light soy sauce, dark soy sauce, essence of chicken and starchy sauce as needed

How to prepare

Step 1

Wash the eggplant and cut into half; use the upper half, do the crisscross cutting from the cut surface down to the top; lay in a dish for later use

Step 2

Spread some salt on the eggplant in the dish and put in a steamer to steam for about 10 minutes on a large flame to be cooked. Take the dish out, and put it on the table.

Step 3

Add hot oil into the wok; add the mashed garlic to stir fry quickly to enhance the flavor. Add in some fresh water and mature vinegar, white sugar, light soy sauce, dark soy sauce, essence of chicken and salt to boil. Add in some starchy sauce to mix well.

Step 4

Serve the mixed sauce on the eggplant and spread on the minced shallot to finish.

- **Ingredients**

common yam rhizome 200g, pre-soaked black fungus 50g, fresh lily bulbs 30g, medlar 1g and minced shallot as needed

- **Seasonings**

salt 4g, cooking wine 3ml, oyster sauce 3g, essence of chicken 3g, potato starch, sesame oil and cooking oil as needed

How to Prepare

Step 1

Peel and wash the yam rhizome and cut into slices. Cut the cleaned black fungus into small pieces.

Step 2

Get a big bowl and put in the black fungus and yam rhizome and then the washed fresh lily bulbs and medlar. Add in oyster sauce, salt, essence of chicken and cooking wine and stir well. Add in some potato starch and mix well. Drip in some sesame oil to stir well.

Step 3

Put the stirred food items in a dish and put in a steamer; cover to steam on a large flame for 7 minutes to be fully cooked.

Step 4

Uncover the steamer and get out the cooked yam rhizome, lily bulbs, black fungus and medlar. Spread on the minced shallot and then serve on some hot oil to finish.

Cooking Time	Taste	Culinary Art	Benefits	Suitable for
7 Minutes	Plain	Steaming	Beauty and Rejuvenation	Female

Steaming Common Yam Rhizome with Lily Bulbs

Tomato and Spinach Soup

Cooking Time	Taste	Culinary Art	Benefits	Suitable for
3 Minutes	Plain	Boiling	Heat-clearing and Detoxification	General

• Ingredients
spinach 200g, tomato 100g, a little sliced ginger

• Seasonings:
salt and essence of chicken as needed

How to prepare

Step 1
Cut the washed tomato into chunks, and the washed spinach into sections.

Step 2
Add an appropriate amount of fresh water in the wok. Add in cooking oil, salt, and essence of chicken after boiling it. Put in the prepared ginger slices.

Step 3
Put in the tomato to boil and the spinach later, to boil for about 2 minutes to be fully cooked.

Step 4
Ladle out in a bowl to finish.

MUSHROOMS

Fried "Chicken-leg" Mushrooms

Cooking Time	Taste	Culinary Art	Benefits	Suitable for
25 Minutes	Plain	Frying	Boost Immunity	Children

• Ingredients
minced pork 100g, coprinus comatus ("chicken-leg" mushroom) 350g, sliced ginger 15g, shallots knot as needed

• Seasonings
salt, white sugar, essence of chicken, light soy sauce, oyster sauce, cooking wine, starch and starchy sauce as needed

> **CULINARY TIPS**
>
> During the frying of the "chicken-leg" mushrooms, the flame should not be strong, in that case the meat will be over-fried.

How to prepare

Step 1

Wash the "chicken-leg" mushrooms and cut into rectangular slices.

Step 2

Add fresh water into the wok and bring to boil and add the "chicken-leg" mushrooms for quick-boiling. Ladle out the boiled "chicken-leg" mushrooms.

Step 3

Add on the minced pork with salt, white sugar, essence of chicken and light soy sauce to pickle for 10 minutes.

Step 4

Add hot oil into the wok and then put in sliced ginger and shallots knot to stir fry quickly to enhance the flavor. Add in cooking wine and fresh water. Add the "chicken-leg" mushrooms, and add in essence of chicken, salt and oyster sauce to boil for 2 minutes. Ladle out the mushrooms and drain off.

Step 5

Pave on a dish with a layer of starch and lay on the "chicken-leg" mushrooms, and then spread on starch even. Serve the minced pork on each slice of the mushroom.

Step 6

Put each slice of the mushroom well and serve on the minced pork separately. Put on a dish for later use.

Step 7

Flip over the dish and move the materials carefully into a wok, the mushrooms should be on top and the meat at the base. fry for 2 minutes until the mushrooms turn golden-brown. Plate up and arrange well.

Step 8

Leave some oil in wok and add in water, oyster sauce, salt, essence of chicken and starchy sauce to stir well to make thick sauce.

Step 9

Serve the thick sauce on the dish and finally spread on minced shallot to finish.

Straw Mushrooms Mixed with Celery

Cooking Time	Taste	Culinary Art	Benefits	Suitable for
4 Minutes	Plain	Mixing	Boost Immunity	General

• Ingredients
straw mushroom 250g, celery 150g, red pepper 10g

• Seasonings
salt 6g, essence of chicken 2g, white sugar 2g, light soy sauce and cooking wine each for 5ml, sesame oil 3ml and cooking oil as needed

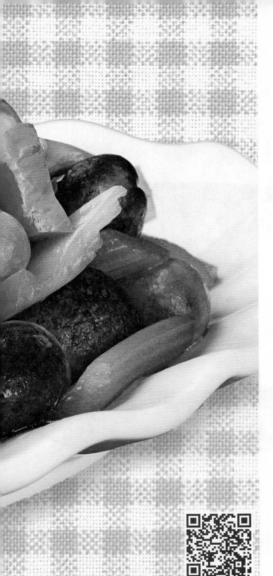

Step 1

Wash the red peppers and cut in half from the top and remove the seeds; and then cut into small pieces for later use. Wash the celery and remove the old stalk, and then cut into sections of 2cm long. Cut off the roots of the cleaned straw mushrooms.

Step 2

Add fresh water into the wok and bring to boil ; add some cooking wine, salt, essence of chicken and cooking oil. Add the straw mushrooms to boil for about 2 minutes until cooked.

Step 3

Add in the celery and red pepper to go on boiling for about half a minute so it's just cooked. Ladle out the boiled materials and put in a dish to cool down.

Step 4

Get a big bowl and put in the boiled mixture. And then add in some light soy sauce, salt, essence of chicken, white sugar and sesame oil.

Step 5

Stir well with chopsticks. Plate up to finish.

CULINARY TIPS

Straw mushroom cooks fresh and delicious; during the cooking don't put too much MSG or essence of chicken, it may spoil the original freshness and the flavor.

Chicken Shreds Soup with Needle Mushrooms

Cooking Time	Taste	Culinary Art	Benefits	Suitable for
4 Mintues	Plain	Boiling	Improve Vitality and Nourish the Blood	Female

• Ingredientsv
needle mushroom 300g, chicken breast 250g, sliced ginger 10g, and minced shallot 10g

• Seasonings
salt, MSG, essence of chicken, starchy sauce and cooking oil as needed

How to prepare

Step 1

Wash the chicken breast and cut into shreds. Add some salt, MSG and essence of chicken to the chicken shreds and knead well. Drip in some starchy sauce to stir well. Add a little cooking oil to preserve the taste.

Step 2

Drain off the water of the cleaned needle mushrooms for later use.

Step 3

Heat up some oil in the wok and add an appropriate amount of fresh water. Put in sliced ginger, and boil with a large flame. Add in salt, MSG and essence of chicken to season well.

Step 4

Put in needle mushrooms and bring to boil, and then put in the chicken shreds, stir while boiling until the mixture is fully cooked.

Step 5

Plate up and spread on the minced shallot to finish.

CULINARY TIPS

Needle mushrooms are tender and delicate, if boiled with a large flame it will spoil the contained nutrients, therefore, it is better to boil with medium flame. In addition, the roots of the needle mushroom are inedible, and should be cut off when washing the mushrooms.

Fish Ball Soup with Two Sorts of Mushrooms

Cooking Time	Taste	Culinary Art	Benefits	Suitable for
6 Minutes	Fresh and Delicious	Boiling	Boost Immunity	Pregnant and Lactating Mothers

• Ingredients
slices of "chicken-leg" mushrooms 35g, slices of straw mushrooms 35g, fish balls 120g, sliced ginger, cilantro and sliced carrots as needed

• Seasonings
salt, essence of chicken, white sugar, scallion oil and soup-stock as needed

How to prepare

Step 1

Add an appropriate amount of soup-stock into the wok, and add the sliced ginger and the sliced carrots and bring to boil.

Step 2

Add slices of "chicken-leg" mushrooms, slices of straw mushrooms and the fish balls and stir well. Boil for about 3 minutes to cook then and add in salt, essence of chicken and white sugar, stir well and season up.

Step 3

Use a ladle to skim off the unwanted greases on the surface of the soup. Drip in some scallion oil and stir well.

Step 4

Ladle out into a bowl and put in the washed cilantro to finish.

CULINARY TIPS
After the boiling of fish balls, you can spread in some chili powder to make the soup more delicious.

SWEETS

Corn Congee with Chestnuts

Cooking Time	Taste	Culinary Art	Benefits	Suitable for
35 Minutes	Sweet	Boiling	Boosts Immunity	General

• Ingredients
yam 100g, chestnuts 50g, smashed corn niblets 50g

• Seasonings
white sugar 40g

How to prepare

Step 1

Wash the chestnuts and cut into small pieces; wash the yam, peel it and cut into dices to use later.

Step 2

Pour 900ml of fresh water in to the wok and bring to boil and put in the smashed corn niblets; cover the wok and use a low flame to boil for about 20 minutes.

Step 3

Uncover the wok and Add the prepared yam and chestnuts, and stir well. Cover the wok and turn to small flame to boil for about 10 minutes until the mixture is fully cooked.

Step 4

Add some white sugar into the wok and stir well, boil until the sugar dissolves completely. Serve in a bowl to finish.

• Ingredients
watermelon 200g, longan pulp 50g, glutinous rice 150g, rice 30g

• Seasonings
white sugar 40g

How to Prepare

Step 1
Cut the watermelon into small pieces, and put on a dish for later use.

Step 2
Add 1000ml of fresh water into the pot and bring to boil. Put in the washed and pre-soaked glutinous rice, and the rinsed rice to stir well.

Step 3
Cover the pot and leave to boil; use a low flame for about 40 minutes, until the rice miz is fully flaccid. Uncover the pot and add some white sugar, mix well.

Step 4
Add in longan pulp and stir well, add the pulp of watermelon; boil for a while before turning the flame off, and enjoy the dish.

Cooking Time	Taste	Culinary Art	Benefits	Suitable for
45 Minutes	Sweet	Boiling	Improve Vitality and Nourish the Blood	Female

Glutinous Rice Congee with Watermelon and Longan

Banana in Hot Toffee

Cooking Time	Taste	Culinary Art	Benefits	Suitable for
4 Minutes	Sweet	Deep-frying	Appetizing and Helps Digestion	General

• Ingredients
banana 200g, flour 140g, one egg, potato starch and custard powder as needed

• Seasonings
white sugar and cooking oil as needed

How to prepare

Step 1
Peel the banana and cut it into small sections; put on a dish for later use.

Step 2
Add in flour with potato starch and custard powder; crack in an egg and add in some fresh water; blend into a paste, then add some cooking oil and stir well.

Step 3
Dip the banana pieces in the flour paste.

Step 4
Add oil to the wok and heat up to 50%-60% of the oil temperature; put the bananas, and use a low flame for deep-frying for about 2 minutes until the bananas turn golden to ladle out.

Step 5
Leave some oil in the wok and add in some fresh water; add in an appropriate amount of white sugar, and stew with low flame, meanwhile, constantly stir clockwise.

Step 6
when the syrup thickens and the colour turns red add the deep-fried bananas and stir quickly.

Step 7
Plate upto finish.

CULINARY TIPS

Bananas contains abundant proteins, fat, carbohydrate, coarsefiber, calcium, phosphorus, iron, as well as carotene, vitamin C, vitamin E and other nutrients. Eating bananas can clear heat and lubricate the intestines, aids digestion, boost immunity, reduce blood pressure, enhances beauty and skin protection.

Lucky Pumpkin Balls

Cooking Time	Taste	Culinary Art	Benefits	Suitable for
2 Minutes	Sweet	Deep-frying	Appetizing and Digestion	Children

• Ingredients
cooked pumpkin 500g, bradcrumbs 100g

• Seasonings
salt 3g, essence of chicken 2g, cooking oil and potato starch as needed

How to prepare

Step 1

Mix the cooked pumpkin with salt and essence of chicken, stir well, and then add in the potato starch to make the pumpkin paste.

Step 2

Knead the pumpkin paste into balls, and dress with breadcrumbs evenly and put them on a dish.

Step 3

Add some oil in the wok to heat up to 40% of the oil temperature, and then put in the pumpkin balls. Deep-fry in a low flame for about 2 minutes.

Step 4

Ladle out the fried pumpkin balls and plate up to finish.

CULINARY TIPS

During making the pumpkin paste, you can put the raw pumpkin in the wok and add water to boil. Cook until the pumkins are fully flaccid, use a spatula or ladle to smash it into paste, and then use a low flame to boil and spread in flour slowly and evenly, and use chopsticks to scramble up, in case that the flour cakes. When the paste becomes thick and condensed, use a large flame to boil, so that the pumpkin paste is flavorful and glutinous.